To all thos
life is too h
to be impossible to live.

To the Holy Spirit for His continual revelations that prove that we could have never accomplished this without Him being the True Author.

To Jesus for making this all possible through the ultimate sacrifice that He made. The only One Who has ever lived the Christian life perfectly! He wants to continue to live His Life through each one of us!

To The Father, our God, for Your lavished gift of Your Only Begotten Son and Your Holy Spirit, Who is ever-present. Thank You for loving us so much.

"*25 to the only God our Savior be glory, majesty, power and authority, through Jesus Christ our Lord, before all ages, now and forevermore! Amen.*" **Jude 1:4**

Acknowledgements

A special thanks to my bride Julie for being a constant inspiration to me and who has believed in and prayed for me, to never doubt what our Father has called me to Be and do during this time in history.

Thanks to my three awesome children, Nicole, Branden and Bobby, who have been so encouraging and fun for me, while always being a constant reminder of God's unconditional love and mercy in my life.

I would like to thank my partner and colleague Sam Gambina. His contribution of editing, writing and collaboration on this project is nothing less than a labor love that has wonderfully blessed many lives.

A special thanks to my friend Brian Solik for his labor of love in writing "The Story of the Bible." Brian's original material was the inspiration behind adapting and writing "A Love Letter From God. It expounds on the materials with a focus of God's grace for salvation and for living founded in the centrality of the Cross of Christ.

A special thanks to the precious churches I have been privileged to pastor over the years. You have been one of the joys of my heart. Without you A Love Letter From God, would not be what it is today.

A Love Letter From God
Living From His Life International
Copyright © 2015 by Bobby Allen

To order other Living From His Life resources, books, teaching CD's, discipleship materials or training guides contact Living From His Life International at 214.934.0741 or email at leadingngrace@gmail.com. You may also visit our website at www.livingfromhim.com

Introduction

Remember what it felt like to receive that letter from your special someone? How you couldn't wait to tear open the envelope so you could not only read the letter but experience the love that you could feel dripping off each page. In the same way, enjoy this love letter from God to you.

Whether you're a new believer or a seasoned follower of God, with every chapter from Genesis to Revelation you'll discover a journey that leads to His heart, character and nature, as He comes alive in every story. He will also reveal to you a common thread throughout biblical history of His plan to usher in the believer's identity in Christ and the grace of God for living. The result? A life of freedom, so that you can experience living the abundant life that Jesus promised!

This book and the leader's guide and study guide have been used as a tremendous blessing for church Sunday school lessons, staff leadership training, youth group curriculum, men and women's bible studies, etc.

"I have been crucified with Christ; and it is no longer I who live, but Christ lives in me; and the life which I now live in the flesh, I live by faith in the Son of God, who loved me and gave Himself up for me." **Galatians 2:20**

Table of Contents
Chapters

CHAPTER 1
The Bible; God's Love Letter

Deuteronomy 29:29; Colossians 1:25-26;
2Timothy 3:16; Hebrews 1:1-2 & 4:12;
2Peter 1:16-18; 20-21; Luke 1:1-4

In his book, *Is The Bible True*, Jeffery L. Sheller says, "The Bible is often described as a timeless book, as one that speaks eternal truths to every age and to every generation, its abiding wisdom resonating across centuries and cultures, inspiring hope in those who read it with faith." If we think about the impact the Bible has made universally in its message on so many people's lives for more than 2000 years, we can see that no book can be judged more timeless.

His love letter is comprised of a rich assortment of literature types hymns and histories, laws and genealogies, prophecies and proverbs, parables and prayers, epistles and apocalyptic visions. I like to think of the Bible as God's love letter to all people. Have you ever received a letter from that special loved one? Remember how excited you were to read it? While reading it, you could actually feel the words on the page comfort you like a warm blanket on a cold night. In the same way, God's love letter tells the story of His relationship with humankind - a relationship that has been both beautiful and tragic.

The Bible is also God's revelation to people. In other words, through the Bible, God reveals Himself to us. God wants all people to learn about Him through this love letter. In this way, we can know Him personally and experience an eternal life with Him, both in heaven, and now on earth. When God exchanges our old life for

Jesus's Life, from that very moment, we have Eternal Life! That is, the Life of His Son living in us and through us. He loves us so much, that He devised a way of making it possible to live with Him and enjoy our relationship with Him for all eternity! The price was His only begotten Son, Jesus. **John 3:16-18**

God has not revealed Himself to people only through the written Word. He has personally visited the planet and interacted with people. In fact, Jesus was God in human form, walking the earth, so that He could relate to us on that level. God inspired about 40 men; over a period of 1600 years, to write down the things He said and did, all in 66 individual letters. What is amazingly interesting is that these men had different personalities, backgrounds, races, cultures, customs, and they were even from different generations. Yet, even now, the Bible maintains its purity and reliability because God wanted His children to know how much He loved them.

These 66 letters make up the Bible, consisting of the Old and New Testaments. He has carefully preserved the Bible over many centuries so that people can come to know Him personally. The Bible has more historic proof of its authenticity than any other literary piece in the world. Thank God that He has revealed Himself to us, both in person and in His Word!

God's Word is also true because He authored it. It has been said that men wrote the Bible. In part, that is true. However, it is more accurately said that Father wrote through them. The word for this is "inspiration". God used each writer's personality, temperament, abilities and talents. Only the Bible has the ultimate truth on God, man and their relationship. God's Word is also without error. The word for this is "inerrancy". Since the Bible is God's Word, and it is true, God alone is man's authority for life. The Bible contains the very wisdom of God Himself.

Overview of the Books of the Bible
Old Testament - 39 Books

LAW - THE PENTATEUCH - 5 BOOKS
These books tell of God's creation of man and the early history of His relationship with people. They also tell of the origin and early history of God's people, the Jews. The books end around 1400BC, with the Jews about to enter Canaan.

Genesis:	Creation, early history of man and Israelites.
Exodus:	God leads Israel out of Egypt and to Mt. Sinai.
Leviticus:	God gives instructions for sacrifices and worship.
Numbers:	God provides for the Israelites wandering in the desert.
Deuteronomy:	God reminds the Israelites of His deliverance and for them to not chase after false gods.

HISTORY - 12 BOOKS
These books continue the story of God's relationship with the Jews. They cover Israel's conquest of Canaan, settlement, division of their kingdom, exile and return. They span almost 1000 years, from ~1400BC - ~450BC.

Joshua:	God leads the Jews in conquering and settling Canaan.
Judges:	God allows different judges to rule the Israelites.

Ruth:	God works through a Moabite woman who exhibits sacrificial love during the time of the judges.
1 & 2Samuel:	God gives Israel kings - Saul, then David.
1 & 2Kings:	Kings lead people astray; the kingdom divides, eventually conquered and exiled as predicted by God's prophets.
1Chronicles:	A selective review of events in 2Samuel.
2Chronicles:	A selective review of events in 1 & 2Kings.
Ezra:	God provides for some exiles to return to Jerusalem and rebuild the temple.
Nehemiah:	God protects the Jews as they rebuild the walls around Jerusalem.
Esther:	A story of courage that takes place among the Jews remaining in Persia.

POETRY - WISDOM - 5 BOOKS

These diverse books include poetry and songs about God, suffering, life, love and wisdom. Other than Job, the poetry books were written mainly during the time of David and Solomon.

Job:	A story about suffering; written during the time of Genesis.
Psalms:	Poetry written by King David and others.
Proverbs:	Wisdom by King Solomon and others.
Ecclesiastes:	Wisdom by King Solomon.
Song of Solomon:	Poetry about love and romance by King Solomon.

PROPHETS

The prophets were God's messengers during the time just before the exile, during the exile and upon return from exile ~800BC - ~400BC. They were used mainly to warn the people of coming judgment and to point them back to God. Many predicted future events, including the coming of the future Deliverer. The prophets are classified as either "major" or "minor" according to the length of their writings.

MAJOR PROPHETS

Isaiah: Messages of judgment but also comfort through the future Deliverer.

Jeremiah: Predicted exile and destruction of Jerusalem and lived to see it happen.

Lamentations: Jeremiah describes the destruction of Jerusalem in emotional poetry.

Ezekiel: God gave visions to Ezekiel, who spoke to the exiles in Babylon and described the coming Deliverer as a shepherd.

Daniel: God works through Daniel in Babylon and Daniel records many prophecies.

MINOR PROPHETS

Hosea: God pictures His faithfulness to Israel in the midst of her spiritual adultery.

Joel: After destruction by locusts, Joel predicts God's further judgment on the Jews.

Amos: Amos rebukes Israel for their materialism, social injustice and false worship.

Obadiah:	Obadiah predicts judgment on Edom, an enemy nation bordering Judah.
Jonah:	Jonah reluctantly spoke of God's grace to the Assyrians, who repented.
Micah:	Micah spoke out against the corruption in both Israel and Judah.
Nahum:	Predicted God's destruction of Nineveh, Assyria's mighty capital.
Habakkuk:	Habakkuk dialogues with God and praises His sovereignty and justice.
Zephaniah:	Judah will be judged on the "Day of the Lord" but blessed in the future.
Haggai:	Encouraged the returning remnant to finish building the Jerusalem temple.
Zechariah:	Encouraged the finishing of the temple and spoke of the coming Deliverer.
Malachi:	Malachi revealed Jews' hypocrisy and told them return to God.

The Books of the Bible

OLD TESTAMENT
39 BOOKS
Law
Genesis
Exodus
Leviticus
Numbers
Deuteronomy

History
Joshua

NEW TESTAMENT
27 BOOKS
Gospels
Matthew
Mark
Luke
John

History
Acts

Paul's Letters
Romans

Judges
Ruth
1 & 2Samuel
1 & 2Kings
1 & 2Chronicles
Ezra
Nehemiah
Esther

Poetry - Wisdom
Titus
Job

Poetry – Wisdom
Philemon
Psalms
Proverbs
Ecclesiastes
Song of Solomon

Major Prophets
Isaiah
Jeremiah
Lamentations
Ezekiel

Prophecy
Daniel
Revelation

Minor Prophets

Hosea	Zephaniah	Obadiah
Joel	Haggai	Jonah
Amos	Zechariah	Malachi

1 & 2Corinthians
Galatians
Ephesians
Philippians
Colossians
1 & 2Thessalonians
1 & 2Timothy

General Letters
Hebrews

General Letters
James
1 & 2Peter
1, 2 & 3John
Jude

Summary

- God is sovereign.

- God is perfect.

- God is love.

- Man is made in God's image.

- Man is valued and loved by God.

- Man was created perfect - without sin.

- Man was created to live in dependence upon God.

- God wants all people to know Him.

- God has revealed Himself through the Bible. The Bible is true and without error.

- People can come to know God through the Bible.

FOR CONSIDERATION

Do you desire to have the word of God, His love letter as your authority for life and ministry? Do you desire to know Jesus as your life, not just as Savior and Lord? If so, please feel free to ask your leaders so that they can walk with you on your journey of discovery.

CHAPTER 2
Angels and Creation

Genesis 1-2 Psalms 8, 104; 148:2,5 Job 38:4-5
Colossians 1:16-17 Hebrews 1:14; 2:16; 12:22;
Matthew 18:10; 24:30-31; 25:41; 28:2; 28:41
Mark 13:32 Luke 1:13-16; 24:4 Acts 12:7-11
2Peter 2:10-11; Ezekiel 28:14, 16-17
Revelation 4:6-11; 12:4,9 Isaiah 14:12,15;
1Peter 1:12; 5:8

Long ago, before the creation of mankind, God created innumerable spirits called angels. The angels were created to serve God and lived in heaven with Him. They were created perfect and holy with great wisdom and strength. Because they are spirits, they do not have a body as humans do, although they may manifest themselves (or show themselves) in bodily form. God's plan was for them to remain with Him in heaven forever.

However, a certain angel named Lucifer, who had a high position among the angels (called a "guardian cherub") rebelled against God and sinned. **Isaiah 14:11-13 (NKJV)** Other angels followed Lucifer in his rebellion. God cast Lucifer and the other angels out of heaven and prepared the lake of fire for them, where ultimately they will be cast with no hope for forgiveness and redemption.

Presently, Lucifer, now called "Satan", (which means adversary or enemy) and the fallen angels (demons) prowl around the earth like a roaring lion fighting against God and His will and trying to influence believers and unbelievers. Believers have victory over Satan's schemes through the Life of Christ. Even so, he can influence them. This is known as walking in the flesh. This is when a Christian tries to do anything by his/her own will while depending on himself/herself rather than Jesus to accomplish it. Unfallen angels serve God in heaven and have a ministry to believers on the earth.

 Then, one day, our Loving Uncreated Creator decided that He would create the heavens the earth and every living thing on the earth, out of nothing. Sound amazing? Can you imagine attempting to create something out of nothing? He simply spoke it all into existence! (i.e. "Let there be light.") Then, after everything was ready, He created man and woman. He placed them in the Garden of Eden. They were different from all of the other creatures He had created. Only Adam and Eve were created in God's image. They were unique - the highest of God's creation. Because they were created in God's image, they were able to think, have emotions and choose.

Adam and Eve are made in God's image. **Genesis 1:27** Since God is Spirit and does not have a physical body, Adam and Eve were not created in God's physical image. "Man was created a rational, moral and spiritual being. He was created in the image of God. In other words, man was created so that he could respond to God. He was endowed with intellect so that he could know God. He was given emotions so he could love God. He was created with a will so that he could obey God." (*Building on Firm Foundations.* Vol. 2, pg. 153)

They were created perfect, which means they were without sin. Imagine waking up every day looking and feeling perfect. If you bumped into Adam in the cool of the day and asked him how he was doing, he would say perfect! How's your wife? Perfect! Adam had no need to lift weights to impress Eve. Eve had no worries about looking to fat or having a bad hair day. Everything about them and their world was perfect!

They enjoyed a love relationship with each other and with God that was endless. God valued them highly, above any other living thing. He placed them as rulers over all of His creation. Imagine receiving such a privileged job from God without needing to prove yourself with an amazing resume or life experience. Your qualifications were simply "I was made by Father."

They also enjoyed a perfect world. There was no sin, sickness nor death. Best of all, they enjoyed a dependent relationship upon a loving God who provided for *all* of their needs even before they knew they had any. They were to multiply the earth with their offspring who would also enjoy this same relationship with each other and God forever. This was God's plan and desire for all mankind. This is a beautiful picture that shows God's amazing love. With this love relationship, God also placed before them the choice of trusting and obeying Him. He warned them that on the day that they disobeyed, they would surely die. The punishment for their sin would be death. The fate of all their offspring lay in their hands.

In today's society it is so different isn't it? People are in a desperate search for personal self-worth. They want to know that their lives count for something, that they are important. This is not a sinful desire, because God created people with a need to be loved and valued. However, God is the only One who can meet this need in Christ His Son. Sadly, most people, even Christians,

11

look instead to worldly things to find worth, significance and security. Whatever makes you feel important is what you depend upon for your self-worth. It may be a career, looks, possessions or intelligence. It may be even seemingly good things, such as Bible knowledge, your dedication to Christ, Christian service, etc. What you turn to in your moment of need could be your god or idol. Turning to the only True God is what is needed.

Other than Father God, if you are finding self-worth out of it, it will define you, confine you and ultimately control you. Why? Because you think you need it to maintain your value or worth to others and to yourself. In other words you may be tempted to believe the lie that your value comes from your valuables, that your self worth equals your net worth. This is also reflected in the saying "Whoever dies with the most toys, wins!" Pretty soon you may find yourself with a deep urge to splurge, which eventually ends with you being possessed by your possessions. At its core, this is known as idolatry - turning to something or someone other than God to get your legitimate needs met in illegitimate ways.

Did you know that God in Christ has freed us from this bondage by revealing that He alone can meet our need to be loved and valued? God gave Adam and Eve a tremendous sense of security and significance by creating them in His image, placing them as rulers over all His creation, caring for all of their needs and initiating a special relationship with them. God actually desired a relationship with His special creation! What a privilege for Adam to know that God created him in order to have a relationship with God Himself and this for all eternity. He learned to live as a loved person. How valuable and loved they must have felt.

When sin came into the world, it polluted all of what Father intended His creation to be. Therefore, the entire universe is out of alignment with God's original design. The fact is that such destructive forces would not come to be if it were not for mankind sinning. It started a whirlwind of destruction not only to mankind but also to nature. Creation was cursed because Adam and Eve listened to the serpent and chose to sin. God's grace is seen even here as He cursed the ground and not Adam directly.

"...in hope that the creation itself will be liberated from its bondage to decay and brought into the freedom and glory of the children of God." **Romans 8:20-21** This shows that Father cares for all created things. He wants the freedom and glory of the children of God to liberate the rest of His creation as well. All things will be set right.

The fact is that Adam and Eve represented all of mankind. We would have done the same thing! Sin has passed down through all generations of those who were born of man. Jesus was not born of the seed of a man but He was *"conceived in her [Mary] ... of the Holy Spirit."* **Matthew 1:20** He had no sin because He was the Son of God. He gained His humanity through the woman. Sin was passed down through the man.

"Therefore, just as through one man sin entered into the world, and death through sin, and so death spread to all men, because all sinned. So then as through one transgression there resulted condemnation to all men, even so through one act of righteousness there resulted justification of life to all men. For as through the one man's disobedience the many were made sinners, even

so through the obedience of the One the many will be made righteous." **Romans 5:12, 18-19**

The seed of the woman is spoken of in Genesis 3:15. *"And I will put enmity between you and the woman, And between your seed and her Seed; He shall bruise you on the head, And you shall bruise Him on the heel."* A woman receives a seed from the man. She does not have a seed but an egg. His seed + her egg = birth of a child. The seed that was received by Mary was the Seed of God. It is because of this Seed, (of the Holy Spirit of God) that Jesus was born without sin.

Both Adam and Eve knew better. **Genesis 3:2-3** *"The woman said to the serpent, "From the fruit of the trees of the garden we may eat; but from the fruit of the tree which is in the middle of the garden, God has said, 'You shall not eat from it or touch it, or you will die.'"* Adam was told directly from God. Eve heard after Adam but they both knew better. They both chose to meet their legitimate needs in illegitimate ways.

"Now the serpent was craftier than any of the wild animals the LORD God had made. He said to the woman, "Did God really say, 'You must not eat (from any tree) in the garden'? The woman said to the serpent, "We may eat fruit from the trees in the garden, but God did say, 'You must not eat fruit from the tree that is in the middle of the garden, (and you must not touch it, God did not say this or you will die).

"The serpent said to the woman, "You surely will not die! For God knows that in the day you eat from it your eyes will be opened, and you will be like God, knowing good and evil." (Truth Twisted - you will be independent of God. You will be under the control of Satan instead of

Father). You may know the difference between good and evil but helpless to do what is good or godly.

Eve was tempted physically, visually, intellectually and spiritually *"When the woman saw that the tree was good for food,* (physically) *and that it was a delight to the eyes,* (visually), *and that the tree was desirable to make one wise,* (intellectually) *she took from its fruit and ate; and she gave also to her husband with her, and he ate. Then the eyes of both of them were opened,* (spiritual revelation) *and they knew that they were naked."* **Genesis 3:6-7**

Now emotionally, intellectually, physically and spiritually vulnerable, they sewed fig leaves together and made themselves loin coverings in order to hide from one another, themselves and God.

Now man is afraid and experiencing full exposure of mind, body and soul. This is when religion was birthed. Now man would always look to find their own way to be pleasing to God based on their performance and trusting in themselves and their own resources. Man would look to earn and achieve God's love and acceptance. The bible calls this living according to the flesh.

"For what the Law could not do, weak as it was through the flesh, God did: sending His own Son in the likeness of sinful flesh and as an offering for sin, He condemned sin in the flesh, so that the requirement of the Law might be fulfilled in us, who do not walk according to the flesh but according to the Spirit. For those who are according to the flesh set their minds on the things of the flesh, but those who are according to the Spirit, the things of the Spirit. For the mind set on the flesh is death, but the mind set on the Spirit is life and peace, because the mind

set on the flesh is hostile toward God; for it does not subject itself to the law of God, for it is not even able to do so, and those who are in the flesh cannot please God. However, you are not in the flesh but in the Spirit, if indeed the Spirit of God dwells in you. But if anyone does not have the Spirit of Christ, he does not belong to Him." **Romans 8:3-9**

"Do not love the world nor the things in the world. If anyone loves the world, the love of the Father is not in him. For all that is in the world, the lust of the flesh and the lust of the eyes and the boastful pride of life, is not from the Father, but is from the world. The world is passing away, and also it's lusts; but the one who does the will of God lives forever." **1John 2:15-17**

The following are ways in which Satan tries to derail Christians and keep unbelievers in their unbelief.

Luke 8:12 – snatching away the Gospel

2Corinthians 4:3-4 – blinding minds to the Gospel

1Timothy 4:1-3 – indoctrinating in false religion

Ephesians 2:1-3 – promoting a false lifestyle

Ephesians 6:10-18 – waging spiritual warfare

Revelation 12:10 – accusing and slandering

Genesis 3:1-5 – planting doubt

Acts 5:3 – tempting to lie

1Corinthians 7:5 – tempting towards sexual sin

1John 2:15-17; 5:19 – tempting with pre-occupation with this world

Matthew 16:21-23 – tempting towards discouragement

Revelation 2:10 – inciting persecution

2Corinthians 11:13-15; 2Peter 2:1-19 – using false teachers

Matthew 13:38-39 – false disciples

2Corinthians 2:10-11 – promoting division

Revelation 20:3 – deceiving the nations

Summary Doctrinal statements:

Satan and his demons actively fight against God and His will

Satan and his demons actively fight against believers

Satan will ultimately be cast into the lake of fire

The following are the truths that tell us that we have power and authority over Satan, through Jesus.

Hebrews 2:14-15 Freed from the slavery through their fear of death

Colossians 2:9-10 We have been made complete and together with Christ, we are over every power and authority

Ephesians 1:21-22 Jesus is the name that has power over all power, authority, dominion and every name that is spoken

Ephesians 4:26-27 We have power to not allow Satan to have a stronghold in our life

Ephesians 6:10-18 The armor of Christ is for our protection from Satan and the armor is actually Jesus as our covering

James 4:7 We can resist the devil by submitting to God and he will flee from us

2 Corinthians 2:10-11 We are not unaware of Satan's schemes – they are based in unforgiveness

2Corinthians 11:3 Satan can deceive us *only* if we let him

1John 4:4 Greater is God Who is living in us than Satan, "the one who is in the world"

2Thessalonians 3:1-3 Jesus will strengthen us and protect us from Satan

1Peter 5:8-9 Satan prowls around to try to devour us – Be of sober mind so as to resist him

1John 5:18-20 We are in Jesus, so the evil one cannot harm us

Matthew 6:13 Father delivers us from the evil one

Matthew 28:18 All authority in heaven and earth has been given to Jesus and we are in Him

Because Christ has defeated Satan's power, all believers have personal victory over Satan. Believers need to stand firm in God's truth and rely on His power. We believe that Jesus has already won victory and that He actually lives in us. Therefore we live and fight from victory, not for victory!

Angels long to understand God's grace towards mankind because God has never extended grace towards the fallen angels. To the fallen angels, it may be an amazement that God went to such an extent to save fallen mankind. What is it about mankind that God would favor them so highly? There really is no answer, other than that God has chosen to express His grace towards us in Jesus, a fact that melts our hearts in gratefulness to God.

Lucifer's sin was pride and expressed itself in the desire to be like God and independent of God. Satan wanted to exalt himself above God and have God subservient to him! That spirit of independence is what keeps mankind from knowing God today with its roots in the fall of man in Genesis 3

Personal experience.
Satan wants us to either fear him or not believe he exists. Either way, he uses this to keep unbelievers from believing in God. With regard to believers, Satan tries to oppress believers by trying to keep them from realizing and experiencing the truth. That Truth is Jesus Himself. We live from victory, not for victory! Greater is He who is in us than he (Satan) that is in the world! **1John 4:4**

Summary

- God is sovereign.

- God is perfect.

- God is love.

- Man is made in God's image.

- Man is valued and loved by God.

- Man was created perfect - without sin.

- Man was created to live in dependence upon God.

FOR CONSIDERATION

Allow God to remind you that Christ is your Life. Remember to thank Him for how much He values and loves you personally. Thank Him for His victory over Satan, which is our victory in Jesus!

CHAPTER 3
The Fall of Man

Genesis 2:16-17; 3; Ephesians 2:1-3
Isaiah 59:2; Roman's 3:23; 5:12-19; 6:23a;
John 3:16-17

Adam and Eve were living in perfect union with each other and God. They were without sin. They and their offspring could enjoy this existence forever, if they chose to obey God's commands. However, Satan had access to the Garden and deceived Eve. Both she and Adam ate from the Tree of the Knowledge of Good and Evil, willfully disobeying God and rejecting His authority in their lives. Instead, they chose to believe and follow Satan. Tragically, sin and its consequences had entered the world. Man and his world would never be the same. God's curse came upon the world and everything in it.

God fulfilled His promise, that if they sinned, they would surely die. ***Genesis* 2:17** The penalty for sin is death. Adam and Eve received God's discipline for their sin. Death came to them in three different ways:

Physical death: although not immediate, the aging process began and they would certainly die a physical death someday. They could no longer eat from the Tree of Life and live forever. **Genesis 3:19, 22**

Spiritual death: they were separated from God, their source of Life. They now became spiritually dead, because they were no longer in union with God. Instead, Satan and their own selfish desires dominated them. Adam and Eve, along with all their offspring, were now spiritually dead and incapable of pleasing God. Their natures were now sinful. This is the *"sin nature"* discussed in the New Testament, which all people inherit from Adam and Eve. **Genesis 3:23-24**

Eternal death: after dying physically, Adam and Eve would be justly condemned to an eternal separation from God in hell, unless God provided a means of payment and forgiveness. Imagine being separated from all that is good for all eternity. Even now, prior to physical death, all people are blessed with Father's goodness. The only difference between saved persons and unsaved persons is that the saved know who to thank and who is responsible for the blessings; the unsaved, do not.

The curse also involved pain during childbirth for Eve, and harder physical labor for Adam. Adam and Eve's relationship would now involve a power struggle. The ground, serpent and all creation were cursed, although Adam and Eve were not cursed. They were disciplined as it were. In general, the perfect world of the garden was now thoroughly corrupted.

Because of Adam's sin, all mankind no longer looked to God for Life. He looked to knowledge for life because that's all that was available until his rebirth. From physical birth, man started to learn how to get what he wanted. He learned how to avoid pain, how to walk independent of God and began to live out of his own resources. He had legitimate needs but he strived to meet them in illegitimate ways. Instead of trusting a loving Father for His provision, he trusted himself and others!

God created man with certain basic needs so that he could experience being a healthy human. Among them are the need to be loved, accepted, to have security, value and worth. The moment you are born, you are driven to get these needs met. The unique ways in which you try to meet your basic God-given needs for love, acceptance, value and worth is your "flesh." Your particular versions of flesh are the unique ways that you have lived by depending on yourself to meet your needs. Your flesh "patterns" were developed based on the messages that you received about yourself as you were growing up. These messages helped form your "identity."

The flesh is you trying to meet your needs independent of Christ with the only resources you have available to you: your mind, will, emotions and your physical body. The flesh is the primary thing that hinders us from knowing and experiencing the victorious Christian life. Living in the flesh is also known as the self-life.

We are all born in Adam, that is, born without the Life of God living in our spirits. Therefore we are spiritually dead to God, and we are forced to live out of our own resources. As a result of dealing with the impossibility of getting our needs met, we are driven to make up for this deficiency. The desire to have our needs met is so great that it consumes our energy; we become solely focused on that longing. We become thoroughly and intensely self-centered in our quest for love, acceptance, value and significance.

The final result of being born spiritually dead is the loss of identity. We were created to have the Life of God within us, (in our human spirit) yet we are brought into the world without it. Therefore, our very reason for existence is not apparent to us. We are born in a condition of not knowing who we are, but being driven to find out.

There are only two kinds of inner life, Adam-life or Christ-Life. **Romans 5:14-19** All of us are born with Adam-life, a spirit without the Life of God. It was the Life of God that Adam lost in the garden. The Tree of Life is a representation of Jesus. They no longer had access to The Tree of Life. Therefore, our sins are not our only problem, but rather the dead spirit within us. The blood of Christ washes away our sin but it does not wash away the Adam life.

The Adam-life had to be put to death so that the Christ-Life would replace it. This was accomplished by what Jesus did on the cross. He became sin for us. **2Corinthians 5:21** That is, we (our sin nature and identity apart from Jesus) were crucified with Christ. **Galatians 2:20**

The Adam-life was gone forever, never to return. The main issue is that we all were born with a spiritual problem. In fact, we were born with two problems. First we were separated from God because of our sin and did not have Life. Yes, we have physical life and our souls were functioning, but we were separated from God. We needed Jesus to be our Life. Second, we need to be delivered from who we are. Our old identity!

Isaiah 59:2 reads, *"But your iniquities have made a separation between you and your God, and your sins have hidden His face from you so that He does not hear."*

Ephesians 2:1-3 reads, *"And you were dead in your trespasses and sins, in which you formerly walked according to the course of this world, according to the* *prince of the power of the air, of the spirit that is now working in the sons of disobedience. Among them we too all formerly lived in the lusts of our flesh, indulging the desires of the flesh and of the mind, and were by nature children of wrath, even as the rest."*

So man's basic problem at birth is that he is separated from God and therefore, without Life. No longer would they or their offspring enjoy the relationship that God had initiated with them in the Garden. Despite their attempt, Adam and Eve were unable to cover their sin or make themselves acceptable to God. Father showed them a picture of the coming answer to their problems. He covered them with animal skins. This is a picture of what the coming Deliverer would do for them. He would cover and forgive their sins. His blood (the life is in the blood) would be given to pay for their sins. He would become their life.

"And according to the Law, one may almost say, all things are cleansed with blood, and without shedding of blood there is no forgiveness." **Hebrews 9:22**

"For the life of the flesh is in the blood, and I have given it to you on the altar to make atonement for your souls; for it is the blood by reason of the life that makes atonement." **Leviticus 17:11**

Their natures were now sinful and self-serving, under Satan's influence instead of God's. All of their offspring would inherit this sinful nature and be born separated from God. There was now a desperate need for a Deliverer to save Adam, Eve and all their descendants from eternal punishment in hell for their sin.

God gave a promise that He would send a future Deliverer. In the midst of disciplining Adam and Eve, God again showed that He is loving, merciful, gracious and forgiving by promising that an offspring of the woman would one day defeat Satan. In the wake of tragedy, God gave a picture of hope. **Genesis 3:14-15**

Do you see that their worth and value came from God? They had value because God valued them. God did not value them because of who they were. He valued them because of who He is. God is Love. **1John 4:16.** They did not have to work for it, earn it or look for worth or value. They had it. They already had value the moment He created them. The same is true for people today. In spite of their sin, God values them because they are His special creation, made in His image. He values all people, even unbelievers. **John 3:16-17**

That's why He desires all of them to be saved. The fact that God went so far as to send His only Son, Jesus, to die for us, should convince us forever of how much God loves us. If God loves unsaved people in this manner, how much more does God love and value those who are His forgiven children. We all get to look to God alone to meet our need to be loved and valued. To look anywhere else is to stoop to a lower level and to consider God's love for us as relatively unimportant. Again, this is called idolatry.

Does this sound extreme and unfair? The reason one might view God's punishment as unfair or too harsh is because we do not have an accurate view of God's holiness and the depth of Adam and Eve's sin. Most people in the world believe in the inherit goodness of man - humanism. God's Word says, *"...for all have sinned and fall short of the glory of God..."* No one is inherently good. Adam and Eve ate from the Tree of The Knowledge of Good and Evil. They knew, as do we, the difference between good and evil. And yet, we choose evil. We try to live life apart from our Father. It is impossible!

"as it is written, There is none righteous, not even one; There is none who understands, There is none who seeks for God. All have turned aside, together they have become useless. There is none who does good; there is not even one. Their throat is an open grave. With their tongues they keep deceiving. The poison of asps is under their lips. Whose mouth is full of cursing and bitterness. Their feet are swift to shed blood. Destruction and misery are in their paths. And the path of peace they have not known. There is no fear of God before their eyes." **Romans 3:10-18, 23**

The important thing to remember is that in the midst of Adam and Eve's rebellion, God was just, but also loving, gracious and merciful. He could have destroyed them all together. But instead, He provided a way of escape through His Son, Jesus.

Satan would now have dominion over the earth. In **Isaiah 14:12-14** we read what Father says about Satan.

"How you have fallen from heaven, O star of the morning, [Lucifer] son of the dawn! You have been cut down to the earth, You who have weakened the nations! But you said in your heart, 'I will ascend to heaven; I will raise my throne above the stars of God, and I will sit on the mount of assembly In the recesses of the north. I will ascend above the heights of the clouds; I will make myself like the Most High.'"

And in **Ezekiel 28:12-17** we read: *"Son of man, take up a lamentation over the king of Tyre and say to him, 'Thus says the Lord GOD, 'You had the seal of perfection, full of wisdom and perfect in beauty. You were in Eden, the garden of God. Every precious stone was your covering, the ruby, the topaz and the diamond; the beryl, the onyx and the jasper; the lapis lazuli, the turquoise and the emerald; and the gold, the workmanship of your settings and sockets, Was in you. On the day that you were created, they were prepared. You were the anointed cherub who covers, and I placed you there. You were on the holy mountain of God. You walked in the midst of the stones of fire. You were blameless in your ways. From the day you were created until unrighteousness was found in you. By the abundance of your trade you were internally filled with violence, And you sinned; Therefore I have cast you as profane from the mountain of God. And I have destroyed you, O covering cherub, from the midst of the stones of fire. Your heart was lifted up because of your beauty; you corrupted your wisdom by reason of your splendor. I cast you to the ground. I put you before kings, that they may see you.'"*

In his arrogance, Satan wanted God's place of rule. Father even showed mercy to Satan. Instead of destroying him, Father allowed him to rule over the earth as the prince of the power of the air. **Ephesians 2:1-2** One day, God's mercy will have had its completion and Satan will be dethroned forever.

A natural question to ask is why the entire human race is under condemnation for the sin of two people. **Romans 5:12-19** provides the answer. One view of this passage, the Representative View, sees Adam as the representative of all mankind. Although Adam sinned, any one of us would have sinned in the same way. Another view, the Seminal View, explains that all mankind sinned when Adam sinned because in some sense, all mankind was present in Adam, when he sinned. As one who was to *"Be fruitful and multiply, and fill the earth, and subdue it;"* we were present in the reproduction process because, though distant, we were the offspring of Adam according to the flesh. **Genesis 1:28** Even if this explanation does not answer all of one's questions; we must remember that God is always just.

What's so encouraging about this story is that God seeks after sinners. God knew that Adam and Eve had sinned, since He is omnipresent and omniscient. Still, He sought after them and approached them, giving them an opportunity to repent **Genesis 3:8-11.** Think about it, God could have justly punished Adam and Eve through immediate physical death and eternal punishment in hell. Instead, He promised a future Deliverer for them and their offspring. **Genesis 3:15**

He also provided an acceptable covering for them. **Genesis 3:21** This covering of skins came through the death of animals. It is significant because it is the first time any physical death has occurred. It also foreshadows God's plan to save sinners by having someone else die in the sinner's place - substitutionary death.

In this case, it is an animal. Later in the Old Testament, lambs and goats were regularly killed to picture a substitute death for the sinner. All of these deaths point towards the ultimate substitutionary death of Jesus, the Deliverer. The covering of Adam and Eve is a picture of how Jesus being sacrificed, covers our sins. Death is always the cost of sin.

All throughout history, in every generation, God will reject man's attempts to cover his sin. Since sinners can do nothing to make themselves acceptable to God, God will reject all of man's efforts to cover his sin. God alone can and will provide an adequate covering.

Adam and Eve sinned for the first time when they chose to disobey God. They believed and followed Satan rather than God. They were no longer perfect and without sin, naked and unashamed. They became aware of their vulnerability (nakedness) and sought to protect themselves by covering their sin and by covering their bodies. Aware of their sin, they feared God and hid from Him. **Romans 5:12-19** shows us how Adam's sin is passed on to all his descendants.

Adam and Eve were unable to cover their sin and make themselves acceptable to God. Their attempts to cover their bodies were rejected by God. **Genesis 3:21** No one can remain or be in God's presence unless they are holy or perfect. Adam and Eve were removed from the garden and God's presence.

Genesis 3:23-24 When a person becomes a Christian, they receive a new nature and no longer have a "sin nature." It was crucified with Christ. **Galatians 2:19-21, Romans 6:5-7** In the New American Standard Version of the Bible, it correctly shows "flesh" rather than "sin nature." The two must not be confused.

"You see, at just the right time, when we were still powerless, Christ died for the ungodly. Very rarely will anyone die for a righteous person, though for a good

person someone might possibly dare to die. But God demonstrates His own love for us in this: While we were still sinners, Christ died for us." **Romans 5:6-8**

Sin cannot separate us from God's love. It didn't before we were saved and it doesn't after we are saved. Father does not look at our actions but at our identity. All of our sins, past, present and future, were removed by Jesus blood - death was paid on our behalf. Father relates to me based on who I am as a new creation spirit.

Summary

- God seeks after sinners.

- God is holy, righteous and demands death as the penalty for sin.

- God is loving, merciful, gracious and forgiving.

- Unsaved man is a sinner and cannot make himself acceptable to God.

- No one can remain or be in God's presence unless they are holy (perfect).

- Satan actively fights against God and against followers of God **Genesis 3:1-5, 15.**

- Satan will be defeated**.**

FOR CONSIDERATION

Allow God to remind you that He is your Life this week by focusing on how He has sought after you and has been loving, merciful, gracious and forgiving to you in spite of your sin.

CHAPTER 4
Noah's Ark

Genesis 3:14-15; 6:1-9; 9:17; Leviticus 17:11;
Psalm 26:1; 101:2; 119:1; 130:3; 143:2;
Matthew 24:37-39; Romans 3:10; 3:23; 5:6-8; 6:23;
1Thessalonians 2:10; Titus 1:6;
Hebrews 10:1-4; 11:6-7; 2Peter 2:4-5

After Adam and Eve sinned, they were removed from the Garden of Eden and from fellowship with God. Now living outside of the garden, separated from God and spiritually dead (unable to live righteously), they began to have children. Eve gave birth to Cain and Abel as well as other children. All of Adam and Eve's descendants were born separated from God. Imagine what it would be like for Adam and Eve to have had a relationship with Father that was so intimate, only to lose it due to sin. Their descendants were born with a sin nature; were spiritually dead and lived under Satan's influence. Unless God provided a way of deliverance, all people would be condemned to die an eternal death in hell for their sinful nature.

Through the years, the earth became more populated and sin ruled mankind, as people were caught in the trap of self-life and Satan's ways. *"Then the LORD saw that the wickedness of man was great on the earth, and that every intent of the thoughts of his heart was only evil continually. The LORD was sorry that He had made man on the earth, and He was grieved in His heart."* **Genesis 6:5-6** God decided to send a flood upon the earth to destroy all mankind. However, a man named Noah and his family found grace in the eyes of the Lord.

Noah was upright in character but was still a sinner in need of forgiveness. Noah responded to God's grace and God chose him to build a giant ark to save people and animals from the flood. God would punish people for their sin, but He would also provide a means of deliverance. Noah completed the ark after 120 years. This shows how patient and loving God was. Could you imagine being Noah and his family? For 120 years his neighbors probably laughed at him. Daily insults of the type "Hey, Noah where's the water for your boat?" "Hey Noah, think it'll float?" Hey Noah have you gone mad! It must have been unbearable at times.

Noah and his family entered, along with two animals of every kind, as well as some extra animals for sacrifice. Although the people had 120 years to change their minds and believe God, no one aside from Noah and his family did. The floodwaters came and all people and animals not in the ark died. The people had refused to trust God's Word. The penalty for their sin was death.

After a little more than one year, the waters receded and Noah and his family walked safely onto land. Can you imagine what it must have looked like coming off that ark and how emotionally impacting that entire situation had to have been on Noah and his family? They were confined to the Ark for over a year! The sense of freedom and overwhelming appreciation they must have felt when they first stepped onto dry ground! This is a physical example illustrating a spiritual fact. They were saved by grace, God's Grace. He covered them. He protected them. Immediately, Noah offered some animals as sacrifices to God. This shows that Noah recognized that it was God's grace that saved him and his family.

God then set a rainbow in the sky to signify His covenant that He would never again destroy the entire world with a flood. This is the first of several important covenants that God will make with mankind. This covenant is called the *Noahic Covenant.* It was an unconditional covenant, which meant that God would always keep His promise, regardless of whether man was faithful or unfaithful. This is a picture of God's grace in action. God then commanded Noah and his family to multiply and fill the earth. By God's mercy and grace, mankind had a new beginning.

Noah and his family were saved by grace through faith. To understand this, it is critical to understand what **Genesis 6:9** means by *"These are the records of the generations of Noah. Noah was a righteous man, blameless in his time; Noah walked with God."* Does blameless mean that he was without sin? To answer this question, one must look at all of Scripture. There are several instances in both the Old and New Testaments in which people either described themselves as blameless; **Psalm 26:1; 119:1; 1Thessalonians 2:10**; or arc exhorted to be blameless. **Psalm 101:2; Titus 1:6**

However, nowhere does any person ever claim to be completely without sin, except of course in the case of Jesus. In fact, scripture repeatedly affirms the sin and guilt of all mankind; **Psalm 130:3; 143:2; Romans 3:10, 23**. From these verses, it is obvious that to be blameless is not to be equated with sinless perfection. Neither does it mean that someone is not under the penalty of death for his or her sin. **Romans 6:23** Being blameless is always in the context of comparison to one's contemporaries. In **Genesis 6:8** it states that Noah "found favor" or grace, in the eyes of the Lord.

So it is important to note that first and foremost, God extended grace to Noah. Noah was saved by grace through faith. **Hebrews 11:7** This supports the scriptural teaching that all people are in desperate need to have God extend grace to them, since all people are born sinners under the penalty of death for their sins. In fact, the only reason God chose to extend grace to Noah and his family was because of His own faithfulness.

He was being faithful to His promise to send the Deliverer from the seed of the woman, Eve. **Genesis 3:14-15** The only difference between Noah and his family and the others, in terms of being delivered, was his faith in God. Noah and his family believed God. As then so it is today, *"that if you confess with your mouth Jesus as Lord, and believe in your heart that God raised Him from the dead, you will be saved."* **Romans 10:9**

You must believe in the Deliverer. They believed God for the coming Deliverer in their hearts. They believed that God would punish sin and that there was only one way of escape. They put their trust in God by entering the ark. The people who perished refused to believe God and instead trusted in their self-life and in their own judgment. This is another consequence of having eaten of the Tree of The Knowledge of Good and Evil. In essence, "I can manage my own life with no help from God." Life is best when I'm in control God and I do not need You!

Noah's sacrifice of animals was a foreshadowing of the death of Christ. This was first seen when God killed animals to provide a covering for Adam and Eve after they had sinned. They tried to cover their shame with fig leaves. God showed in sacrificing life, although of an animal, that sin ultimately causes the spilling of blood or death. Because all people are under the penalty of death for their sin, part of God's salvation plan is for someone else to suffer death in the sinner's place as a substitute so that the sinner can be freed from his own penalty of death.

Our sin was covered by Jesus' shed blood or death. *" For the life of the flesh is in the blood, ... "* **Leviticus 17:1** This is referred to as "substitutionary death" or "substitutionary atonement". Although the death of animals was never sufficient to remove man's sin, **Hebrews 10:4**, in the Old Testament, it did provide a vivid picture of the death required of all people for their sins and of the people's need for a substitute and an ultimate Deliverer.

When a person offered sacrifices to God in faith, believing that they deserved death for their sins and that God alone could provide forgiveness, God accepted their sacrifices, forgave their sins and accepted them. When Noah sacrificed animals, he was recognizing that he and his family deserved to die in the flood, but that God had graciously spared their lives. Sacrificing the animals showed Noah's faith in God and acknowledged God's provision of deliverance for them.

Although Christ had not yet come to earth, in God's eyes, Jesus Christ had already died for the sins of all people. **Romans 5:6-8** So when someone in the Old Testament came to God in faith, which was usually shown by offering sacrifices, God applied the future death of Christ to them. It was a confession by them that their sin cost life. "This should have been me" and also that "I believe that God will forgive me." The people knew very little about the coming Deliverer, but those who came to God in faith, trusting in God's forgiveness, were accepted and saved by God.

God extended grace to Noah. Noah was saved by grace through faith. **Hebrews 11:7** This supports the scriptural teaching that all people are in desperate need to have God extend grace to them, since all unsaved people are sinners under the penalty of death for their sins.

In fact, the only reason God chose to extend grace to Noah and his family was because of His own faithfulness. He was being faithful to His promise to send the Deliverer from the seed of the woman, Eve. The only difference between Noah and his family and the others, in terms of being delivered, was faith. Noah and his family believed God. They believed that God would punish sin and that there was only one way of escape. They put their trust in God by entering the ark. The people who perished refused to believe God and instead trusted in themselves.

Noah's sacrifice of animals was a foreshadowing of the death of Christ. This was first seen when God killed animals to provide a covering for Adam and Eve after they had sinned. Because all unsaved people are under the penalty of death for their sin, part of God's salvation plan is for someone else to suffer death in the sinner's place.

SUMMARY

- God is holy, righteous and demands death as the penalty for sin.

- God is loving, merciful and gracious.

- Unsaved man is a sinner and cannot make himself acceptable to God.

- Man can come to God only according to God's will and plan.

- The only way to please God is to trust by faith that God is living His life through you.

FOR CONSIDERATION

Allow God to remind you that He is your only Life this week through the truths you learned about His grace to Noah and his family. This same grace is offered to you for salvation and living the abundant life.

CHAPTER 5
The Abrahamic Covenant

Genesis 3:15; 12:1-7; 15:1-6; 16:1-4,15-16; 17:1-27;
Genesis 21:1-5; 22:1-14; John 6:28-30 (NASB);
Romans 4; Hebrews 11:8,12,17-19

Noah's Ark ended with God commanding Noah and his family to multiply and fill the earth. Man began to re-populate the earth and God promised to never again destroy the world with a flood. Some would say isn't this just God starting over? Father showed that rinsing sinners down the drain with their sin was not the answer. The problem was not external, but internal. Sin had to be dealt with on an internal spiritual basis.

Therefore, man was still in desperate need of the coming Deliverer whom God had promised in **Genesis 3:15.** Because they were descendants of Adam, all people were born D.O.A. (dead on arrival) as sinners. They were separated from God and under the penalty of eternal death in hell as punishment for their sins. They were living under Satan's influence, not God's. Yet, in His wonderful grace, God had not forgotten His promise to send the Deliverer who would defeat Satan and free people from the penalty and power of sin.

By His sovereignty, God chose to bring the coming Deliverer into the world through the descendants of one man: Abram. God spoke to Abram, commanding him to leave his country and to settle in the land of Canaan. God promised to bless Abram, to give him countless descendants and to give him the land of Canaan.

In **Genesis 15:6(NIV)** we read that *"Abram believed the LORD, and He credited it to him as righteousness."*

Also, **Romans 4:3,** *even* today, like then, belief in God is the answer. **John 6:28-30** *" Therefore they said to Him, [Jesus] 'What shall we do, so that we may work the works of God?' Jesus answered and said to them, 'This is the work of God, that you believe in Him whom He has sent.'* By our Deliverer living His Life through us, we show who we believe. God also said that all nations of the earth would be blessed through Abram, signifying the worldwide impact of the coming Deliverer.

Abram's descendants would later become known as the nation of Israel, or the Jewish people. Their distinguishing characteristic was that all males were circumcised. Circumcision was a sign of God's unconditional covenant with them called the *Abrahamic Covenant.* Since the Deliverer would be born from Abram's family line, the Deliverer would also be a Jewish male. All of this occurred 2,000 years before the birth of the Deliverer.

God eventually changed Abram's name to Abraham, which means "father of many". However, Abraham grew to be 100 years old and his wife Sarah was 90. At this time, they still had no child. They wondered how God could send the Deliverer into the world through Abraham's family if both he and Sarah were far past childbearing age. Like any of us would have, Abraham and Sarah grew tired of waiting on God and decided to take matters into their own hands (walking in the flesh/being in control). Therefore, Abraham fathered a child, called Ishmael, through Sarah's servant Hagar. However, this was not God's plan. Remember, if you want God's best let Him choose. Instead, in their old age, God did the impossible; He showed His faithfulness and enabled Sarah to bear a child named Isaac.

Years later, God told Abraham to kill his only son Isaac as a sacrifice to Him (His other son Ishmael was not considered a son of the promise that God had made to Abraham). Ishmael is a picture of man trying to accomplish God's purpose through human effort instead of trusting God to fulfill His promise. This is called "walking after the flesh". How could God send the Deliverer through Abraham's bloodline if his only descendant was killed? By God's grace.

God gave Abraham the faith to tie Isaac upon an altar to kill him. At that crucial moment, just before Abraham was going to slay his son, his only son, with a knife, an angel stopped him and seeing a ram (a male lamb) caught in the nearby bushes offered it instead to God. God had provided a substitute. Abraham called that place *"The Lord will provide"* because God had provided a substitute, a ram, a male sheep, to die for Isaac. This is a picture of the coming Deliverer, who would die as a substitute for sinners that they might have Life and know Him as their Life!

Abraham believed God and he showed his trust in God by obeying Him. He showed incredible faith in God by his willingness to sacrifice Isaac. Because he was a descendant of Adam, Abraham was also a sinner in need of God's grace. In **Genesis 12**, he showed he was walking by the flesh by disobeying God when he fathered a child through Hagar and by lying about Sarah being his wife.

Because God commanded Abraham to sacrifice Isaac, Abraham could not have substituted something else for Isaac. Man must come to God only according to God's will and plan. In other words, man must come to God "God's way", not "man's way." Isaac was set free because there was an acceptable sacrifice available in his place. And it was God who provided the sacrifice. This parallels the fact that the coming Deliverer is the only acceptable sacrifice that God can accept as our substitute. Once again, it was God who would provide the acceptable sacrifice for us. Depending on our flesh or our coping mechanisms will never work.

Abraham was typical of people today in that he was a sinner. Abraham trusted in his flesh and therefore impatiently took matters into his own hands, rather than wait upon God's promises. His faith and trust in God sometimes wavered. He was atypical in his response to go to a foreign land with many unknowns in front of him. It was also amazing how he trusted God by his act of faith in offering Isaac to Him.

SUMMARY

- God is faithful to His promises.

- God is holy, righteous and demands death as the penalty for sin.

- God is loving, merciful and gracious.

- Unsaved man is a sinner and cannot make himself acceptable to God.

- Man can come to God only according to God's will and plan.

- The only way to please God is to trust by faith that God is living His life through you.

FOR CONSIDERATION

Allow God to remind you that He is your Life this week by reflecting on His faithful provision for you in the past. Then talk to God about some things you want to trust Him with today.

CHAPTER 6
The Passover

Exodus 1-15; 12:5; Leviticus 17:11;
2Corinthians 12:9; Ephesians 3:14-21;
Philippians 4:13; Hebrews 11:23-29

Several hundred years have passed since the time of Abraham. Abraham's son Isaac had a son named Jacob who had 12 sons. Through the events surrounding one of Jacob's sons, Joseph, all the Jewish people moved to Egypt. Now, beginning in the book of Exodus, the number of Israelites has increased greatly, but the Egyptians have enslaved them cruelly for many years. This sets the scene for God's miraculous display of power and the deliverance of His people from the powerful Egyptian kingdom. God had not forgotten His people and His covenant with Abraham.

God's chosen instrument to lead His people out of Egypt was Moses. He was an Israelite who God sovereignly saved from death as a baby and who grew up in Pharaoh's household. As an adult, he killed an Egyptian and escaped into the desert where he stayed for 40 years. While in the desert, God appeared to Moses in the form of a burning bush. He told Moses that He wanted to use him to redeem the people of Israel from bondage. Moses, however, did not trust totally in God's ability to use him and so his brother Aaron was to be their spokesman.

As with us, Moses was trusting in his flesh by looking to his own abilities to accomplish what God wanted to do through him. When we look to Father for His sufficiency instead of our own, we are walking in the

Spirit of God. We are trusting Father to "pull it off."
Ephesians 3:14-21

In our weakness, Father's strength is better shown. We can't "pull it off." It is more than evident that we can't! It is only by His grace. **2Corinthians 12:9** The only way that we can be strong enough to accomplish anything is in the strength of our weakness. God gives us Himself and through Him we can do anything! **Philippians 4:13**

Moses and Aaron came to Pharaoh for the Israelite's release. But because Pharaoh refused, God sent a series of plagues upon the Egyptians. There were 10 plagues in all: **1)** the Nile turned to blood; **2)** frogs; **3)** gnats; **4)** Flies; **5)** livestock all died; **6)** boils appeared on all animals and Egyptians; **7)** devastating hail fell on the land; **8)** locusts devoured all the crops; **9)** darkness covered the land for 3 days and **10)** the death of the firstborn son.

The plague of death came to all the Egyptian households, but God "passed over" the Israelite households because of their faith in God's word, which was shown by the blood of the lamb placed around their doors. The coming Deliverer would give His blood (Life - in order to pay for our sins) *"For the life of a creature is in the blood..."* **Leviticus 17:11** It was very specific as to what kind of lamb was chosen.

"Your lamb shall be an unblemished male a year old; you may take it from the sheep or from the goats." **Exodus 12:5** This "Passover Lamb" was a picture of the coming Deliverer. He who would also be perfect and innocent (male and without defect - that is, sin) and would die for people so that they could escape God's

punishment and slavery to sin and death for all eternity, in hell.

We see from this story that God is sovereign. He puts on display the fact that He alone controls nature, events and people for His purposes and glory. He declared Himself, as "I am who I am". God punished sin, showing that He is righteous. God demanded a perfect lamb as a sacrifice symbolizing His holiness. God's punishment on the Egyptians showed that ultimately He demands death as the penalty for sin. God showed His personal love for the Israelites by keeping His covenant promises to them. He showed His mercy and grace by providing a way for them to escape punishment through the death of a lamb.

After all the disasters, Pharaoh finally gave permission for Moses to lead the Israelites out of Egypt. Moses was to lead them from Egypt to their homeland, the land promised to Abraham, Canaan. But how could they make the trip? In all practicality the body of the lamb, which they were instructed to eat, would be their sustenance so they would be able to make the journey to the Promised Land. This also was a picture of the coming Deliverer.

Not only would blood be payment for our sins, but the body of the Deliverer would give Life. The Deliverer would be the "sustenance" that would be needed so that humanity could continue in life in route to the new Promised Land - Heaven. In essence, the Deliverer would be our Life! Those who depended solely on the Deliverer for Life, would make the trip. Those who didn't would not.

As Israel traveled to the Promised Land, God guided them by a pillar of cloud by day and a pillar of fire by night. Soon after they left, Pharaoh changed his mind again. He and his army pursued the Israelites. God miraculously parted the Red Sea, bringing the Israelites to safety and destroying Pharaoh and all of his mighty army. God was faithful and brought His people out of slavery and into freedom. He had redeemed Israel.

The Egyptians certainly showed that they were sinners by their selfish and ruthless enslavement of the Israelites, as well as Pharaoh's pride and stubbornness. The Israelites also showed their sin by their quick judgment and impatience with Moses. All of them were sinners by birth because they were all descendants of Adam. Man's inability to save himself is shown by the Egyptians' inability to escape God's judgment and Israel's inability to free themselves from slavery.

God had a specific plan for the Israelites to escape punishment at the Passover and to escape from Egypt. If they had tried to escape Egypt on their own initiative, they would have failed. If they had tried to escape the Passover death by using their own plan and ideas, they would have failed. That is why God told them specifically what they needed to do. They could not simply rely upon their own ideas or strategies on how to be accepted by God and how to escape His punishment.

God's redemption of Israel was not based upon their righteousness. It was based solely upon their faith and trust or belief in God. They had to believe that God would indeed bring death at the Passover and that the only way for them to escape death would be to kill a lamb and spread it's blood on their door. When God saw the blood, He passed over their house. God did not evaluate their righteousness, but instead saw the blood and spared the Israelites from judgment. The blood was a sign of their faith or trust in God and His rescue plan for them. As already mentioned, this pictures the substitutionary death of Christ as our life and Passover Lamb.

SUMMARY

* God is sovereign.

* God is holy, righteous and demands death as the penalty for sin.

* God is loving, merciful and gracious.

* Unsaved man is a sinner and cannot make himself acceptable to God.

* Man can come to God only according to God's will and plan.

* The Law or Ten Commandments exposes people for who they truly are in their flesh.

FOR CONSIDERATION

Allow God to remind you that He is your Life this week by reflecting upon His glory, majesty, power and holiness as seen in this story. The Law or Ten Commandments exposes people for who they truly are apart from Jesus. It shows that condemnation apart from Christ is just. Because of God's merciful grace, we are spared the punishment that we absolutely deserve. Thank Father for His loving kindness, mercy and grace towards you.

CHAPTER 7
The Ten Commandments

Exodus Chapters 19-20; 24:1-8; 32; 34:5-7;
Deuteronomy 28:1-59; Romans 3:9-20; 7:7-13;
Galatians 3:19-25; James 2:10; Hebrews 12:18-24

Several weeks after crossing the Red Sea, Moses and all the Israelites stopped at Mt. Sinai. The Lord planned to enter into another covenant with His people, called the *Mosaic Covenant.* This was different from the one He had made with Abraham. The Mosaic Covenant was a conditional covenant. That is, God would bless the Israelites only if they obeyed Him fully and kept all of the commands of the covenant. *"All the people answered together and said, 'All that the LORD has spoken we will do!'* **Exodus 19:8**

And Moses brought back the words of the people to the LORD. This statement will very soon be what renders them unable to experience God on a personal and intimate level. Over and over again the Israelites would have this as a resounding response to Father throughout their "obedience" history. Over and over again, they failed to live up to what they promised.

Then God told Moses to prepare the people because God Himself was going to descend upon Mt. Sinai and give the terms of His covenant. Until now, God had generally not been physically present among His people. God is holy and cannot be in the presence of sin or sinners under the Old Covenant. God is also righteous and demands death as the penalty for sin. So God commanded the people not to go near the mountain or to touch it. If they did, man or animal, God said that they would die. They were all to remain separate from God, which symbolized their spiritual separation due to sin.

On the morning of God's arrival on Mt. Sinai, there was a thick cloud, thunder, lightning and the sound of a trumpet so loud that the people trembled with fear. There was fire, smoke, the mountain trembled violently and the sound of the trumpet grew louder and louder. Then God spoke to Moses and gave him the terms of the covenant: the Ten Commandments or The Law. These were written on two stone tablets, along with other laws and regulations.

When Moses told the people all of God's words and laws, they once again responded with one voice, *"Everything the Lord has said, we will do."* Moses wrote down everything in the Book of the Covenant. He then confirmed the covenant with God by sprinkling blood from sacrificed animals onto the tablets. God said that He would bless them if they obeyed all of His laws and He would curse them if they disobeyed. The details of these blessings and curses are written in **Deuteronomy 28.**

By replying, *"Everything the Lord has said, we will do,"* the Israelites believed that they could obey Father's Law. But they couldn't. They thought by their own efforts, abilities, strength they would be able to please Father. Even today, both Christians and non-Christians try to be acceptable to God by their own efforts. This is called living after the flesh. If they knew of their desperate need and were being honest with themselves they would reply, "Father, no matter how hard I try, I can't keep Your law. Please have mercy on me."

In **Exodus 33:19** Father says, *"And He said, 'I Myself will make all My goodness pass before you, and will* *proclaim the name of the LORD before you; and I will be gracious to whom I will be gracious, and will show compassion on whom I will show compassion.'" And again He says in* **Isaiah 66:2,** *"For My hand made all these things, Thus all these things came into being,' declares the LORD. 'But to this one I will look, to him who is humble and contrite of spirit, and who trembles at My word.'"*

While Moses went back up the mountain for more instructions, the Israelites grew impatient and rebelled against God and Moses by creating a golden calf to worship. They worshipped the false god by drinking, dancing and disobeying the covenant they had only recently promised to obey. In fact, by building the golden calf, they violated the first commandment. God threatened to kill all of them, but through Moses' intervention of prayer and supplication, God relented.

Still, the sword killed 3,000 and many others were struck by a plague due to their sin. The Israelites had already been unfaithful to the Mosaic Covenant. In essence, instead of moving forward with God, they regressed to the false gods and the worshipping of them. They repeated their sins. They went back to a sin-based lifestyle. In **Proverbs 26:11** we read, *"Like a dog that returns to its vomit is a fool who repeats his folly."*

Many people, saved and unsaved, believe that the only reason God gave the Ten Commandments was to teach people how to live. This is unscriptural. Although the Commandments are good, moral and God did give them to the Israelites, God's primary purpose was entirely different. Until one understands the true purpose of the Law, he will be hopelessly in bondage to trying to obey it through flesh management and survival strategies.

The apostle Paul explains the real purpose of the Law in the verses above. God instituted the Law from the time of Moses until the coming of Christ in order to show God's holiness, man's sinfulness and to lead them to Christ, the coming Deliverer. God used the Law to show the Israelites their sinful nature, their inability to obey God fully and their desperate need for mercy from God. The Law showed the people their need for a Deliverer to come and rescue them from their sins.

It was intended to be a constant reminder to people of their sin. Until the coming of Christ, the people were under condemnation because *"For as many as are of the works of the Law are under a curse; for it is written, 'Cursed is everyone who does not abide by all things written in the book of the law, to perform them.'*
Galatians 3:10

Now that Christ has come, people are no longer under the supervision of the Law. Later in the following chapters, we will find out how Christ fulfilled the Law and why Christians are no longer under the Law. God's purpose was to show His holiness and people's sin, that is why the covenant needed to be demanding. It needed to reflect the perfect holiness of God and the perfect standard God required for people to be in His presence. As it was, the covenant was impossible for the Israelites to keep. If God really expected them to fully obey all His terms, then the covenant would have been too demanding. Although God desired them to fully obey, He knew that they would not be able to do so. The Law served its purpose by showing people their need for a Deliverer to come and rescue them from their sins.

It is common in our human thinking to feel that God was too severe in killing many Israelites for their sin. The reason we usually feel this way is because we have too limited a view of God's holiness and our own sinfulness. We think that God should be able to "overlook" our sin and be a little more lenient. Satan would certainly love for us to believe this lie. This is precisely why we must rely upon the truth of God's Word instead of our own thoughts. God will punish sin and the punishment for sin is always death.

What a loving and kind God that He would initiate a relationship with His people. Just as in the Garden, when God sought after Adam and Eve, in this story, God initiates a covenant with people. He also initiates coming down to them to be in their presence and to continue a relationship with them.

God's holiness and righteousness are shown by the people's need to remain separate from the mountain where He dwelt. His holiness and righteousness are also shown by the strict commandments He gave to them. In order to be in a relationship with Him, the Israelites needed to be as holy as God, represented by total obedience to God's commands. The stern warning of death to those who touched Mt. Sinai shows the punishment of death for sin. This is also shown by the death of many people after the golden calf incident. God showed that He would punish sin by death.

Thankfully, that in the midst of this terrifying scene of God's holiness and wrath, God shows Himself to be loving, merciful and gracious by initiating a relationship and covenant with the Israelites. He chose to live in their midst. He also chose to relent from destroying them all after they sinned. God would have been just if He had destroyed them all. But He remained gracious.

Our feelings should be similar to the Israelites' who trembled with awe and fear. However, **Hebrews 12** paints a completely different picture for Christians. We need not fear God in the same way, but get to worship God with reverence and awe over what He has done through Christ to bring us out from under condemnation and into His grace.

SUMMARY

- God is sovereign.

- God is holy, righteous and demands death as the penalty for sin.

- God is loving, merciful and gracious.

- Unsaved man is a sinner and cannot make himself acceptable to God.

- Man can come to God only according to God's will and plan.

- The Law or Ten Commandments exposes people for who they truly are apart from Jesus. It shows that condemnation apart from Christ is just.

FOR CONSIDERATION

Allow God to remind you that He is your Life this week by reflecting upon His glory, majesty, power and holiness as seen in this story.

CHAPTER 8
The Tabernacle

Exodus 24:12-18; 25:1-33; 26:31-33; 28:1-3; 29:38-46;
Exodus 39:32; 40:33-38;
Leviticus 1:1-5; 16:2-10; 22:17-20; Deuteronomy 4:24;
John 6:49-51; 7:37-39; 12:46;
Hebrews 9:1-22; 10:1-12; 12:28-29

While the Israelites were still camped at Mt. Sinai, God gave Moses specific, detailed instructions for the building of the Tabernacle. This was to be the place where God Himself was to live with the people. God also appointed some to serve full-time in the Tabernacle as priests. Ever since Adam and Eve were separated from God in the garden, God had not lived among people. Because the Israelites were sinners, a holy God could not live among them in the way He originally did with Adam and Eve. There had to be certain regulations and a covering for the people's sin.

God's holiness is seen by the need for Him to be separated from the people and the people's need to be cleansed daily in order to remain in His presence. The entire tabernacle and sacrificial system represent two major truths: God's holiness and man's sin. God's demand for death as the penalty for sin is shown by the daily sacrifices offered to God. The animals were killed signifying that God punishes sin by death.

God's love is shown by His desire to live with His people. His mercy and grace are shown by His acceptance of animal sacrifice instead of requiring the people's own death for their sins. God made a provision for their sin. He could not overlook their sin, but allowed substitutionary sacrifices to be made to atone for or cover their sin.

The construction and items of the Tabernacle have special significance. The *altar of burnt offering* or *brazen altar* was where animals were regularly sacrificed to God. This represented the people's need for substitutionary sacrifices for their sins. The *laver* was the basin of water that the priests used to cleanse themselves. This represented the people's need for cleansing before God. The coming Deliverer would give this cleansing water.

"Now on the last day, the great day of the feast, Jesus stood and cried out, saying, 'If anyone is thirsty, let him come to Me and drink. He who believes in Me, as the Scripture said, 'From his innermost being will flow rivers of living water.' But this He spoke of the Spirit, whom those who believed in Him were to receive; for the Spirit was not yet given, because Jesus was not yet glorified." **John 7:37-39**

The lamp stand or candlestick, which burned continuously, represented the people's need for light in the midst of their spiritual darkness.

"I have come as Light into the world, so that everyone who believes in Me will not remain in darkness." **John 12:46**

The table containing 12 loaves of bread symbolized the spiritual and physical sustenance that only God could give. The 12 loaves also represent the 12 tribes of Israel. Each and every tribe needed the Bread of Life. This is also a picture of Jesus, the future Deliverer, as the Bread of Life.

"'Your fathers ate the manna in the wilderness, and they died. This is the bread, which comes down out of heaven, so that one may eat of it and not die. I am the living bread that came down out of heaven; if anyone eats of this bread, he will live forever; and the bread also which I will give for the life of the world is My flesh.'" **John 6:49-51**

The Bread of Life is that basic food that we need in order to travel through the journey of life. That Bread is Jesus. We need Jesus to sustain us through this life. Apart from Jesus, we would have no life. We would be spiritually dead like those who do not know Him! With Jesus living His Life through us, we would never hunger for true Life. After all, He is our Life our only Life!

"Jesus said to him, 'I am the way, and the truth, and the life; no one comes to the Father but through Me. If you had known Me, you would have known My Father also; from now on you know Him, and have seen Him.'" **John 14:6-7**

The altar of incense, which burned continuously, represented the people's constant need for intercession or prayer on their behalf. This is also a representation of the Holy Spirit interceding for us.

" In the same way the Spirit also helps our weakness; for we do not know how to pray as we should, but the Spirit Himself intercedes for us with groanings too deep for words; and He who searches the hearts knows what the mind of the Spirit is, because He intercedes for the saints according to the will of God." **Romans 8:26-27**

A veil or curtain separated the *Most Holy Place* or *Holy of Holies* from the Holy Place. The Most Holy Place is where God Himself dwelt. The *veil* represented the separation between God and man due to sin.

"And Jesus cried out again with a loud voice, and yielded up His spirit. And behold, the veil of the temple was torn in two from top to bottom; and the earth shook and the rocks were split. The tombs were opened, and many bodies of the saints who had fallen asleep were raised; and coming out of the tombs after His resurrection they entered the holy city and appeared to many. Now the centurion, and those who were with him keeping guard over Jesus, when they saw the earthquake and the things that were happening, became very frightened and said, 'Truly this was the Son of God!'"
Matthew 27:50-54

The veil was torn from top to bottom. This is a picture of the acceptance initiated in heaven and descending to earth. Father initiated the ultimate sacrifice for our sins. He ripped away the separation between mankind and Him by the death of His only begotten Son.

"But their minds were hardened; for until this very day at the reading of the old covenant the same veil remains unlifted, because it is removed in Christ. But to this day whenever Moses is read, a veil lies over their heart; but whenever a person turns to the Lord, the veil is taken away. Now the Lord is the Spirit, and where the Spirit of the Lord is, there is liberty." **2Corinthians 3:14-17**

The *Ark of the Covenant* was a chest with a cover called the *mercy seat*. On top of the mercy seat were two *cherubim* (gold figures with wings) facing each other. God would dwell between these two cherubim and a very bright light would indicate His presence.

This is a picture of God's mercy shining through into our hearts to save us. The Holy of Holies is now contained in those who are saved. The actual God of all creation, the universe and all that is outside of it and inside of it, lives in us. His Spirit is in union with our new spirit that we received when we asked Jesus to be our Savior. That bright Light is dwelling in us and through us as a testimony of God's grace, mercy and love!

"'You are the light of the world. A city set on a hill cannot be hidden; nor does anyone light a lamp and put it under a basket, but on the lampstand, and it gives light to all who are in the house. Let your light shine before men in such a way that they may see your good works, and glorify your Father who is in heaven.'" **Matthew 5:14-16**

The good deeds are Father shining His Life through us. We are reflections of that consuming fire.

"For the LORD your God is a consuming fire, a jealous God." **Deuteronomy 4:24**

"Therefore, since we receive a kingdom which cannot be shaken, let us show gratitude, by which we may offer to God an acceptable service with reverence and awe; for our God is a consuming fire." **Hebrews 12:28-29**

As the sparks of Jesus' love shines through us, others will be ignited with the love of Christ. Let your light shine!

When the Israelites finally finished the precise details of the Tabernacle after 2 years, God's glory filled the Tabernacle as God came down to live in the Holy of Holies. Now that God was actually living in their midst, the people and priests offered sacrifices to God day after day to cover or atone for their sins. The animals that were killed had to be a certain kind and age. They had to be perfect and without any blemish. This is a picture of Jesus as the perfect, sinless sacrifice for all who would trust in Him.

The person was to lay his hand on the animal to be offered signifying that he himself deserved to die for his sins, but that God was allowing the animal to die in his place as a substitute. The priests would then sprinkle the blood around the altar and tent. Although the animal's death really did not pay for the people's sins, they were a picture of the coming Deliverer whose death would be sufficient to pay for all people's sins once and for all. There would be no need to ask for forgiveness once a person became saved. They simply need to agree with God (confess) that their sin (walking in the flesh) was wrong, and thank Him. This is a confession of faith, of the fact that all of their sins were already forgiven the moment they became saved in Christ.

Man's sin is graphically shown by his need for daily atonement and cleansing through the killing of animals. His sin is shown by his separation from God and his inability to cleanse himself from his sins. God gave Moses specific instructions as to the building of the Tabernacle and as to how the Israelites needed to offer sacrifices in order to remain in the presence of a holy God. They could not come to God on the basis of their own initiative, but only according to God's instructions. If anyone other than the high priest tried to enter the Holy of Holies, God said that they would be killed.

The Tabernacle itself represents God's dwelling place. Since Christians actually have God living in them, the Tabernacle can be said to represent the Christian's physical body. **1Corinthians 3:16** The *altar of burnt offering* or *brazen altar* represented the people's need for substitutionary sacrifices for their sins. Christ became the ultimate final sacrifice. **Hebrews 9:28; 10:12-14**

The unblemished *animals* represented the sinless perfection of Christ. The *laver* or *basin* represented the people's need for cleansing before God. Through Christ, people can be cleansed from their sins. **Hebrews 9:14** The lamp stand or *candlestick* represented the people's need for light in the midst of their spiritual darkness. Jesus said He was the light of the world. **John 8:12**

The *table* containing 12 loaves of bread symbolized the spiritual and physical sustenance that only God could give. Jesus said He was the bread of life; **John 6:35**. The *altar of incense* represented the people's constant need for intercession or prayer on their behalf. Jesus interceded for believers before God; **Hebrews 7:25.** The *high priest* represented the people's need for a mediator or representative before God. Christ is now our high priest. **Hebrews 4:14-5:10; 7:23-8:4; 10:19-22** The ceremonial cleansing of the priest represented the sinless perfection of Christ.

The *veil* represented the separation between God and man due to sin. At the moment when Christ died, God tore the veil in the temple from top to bottom, signifying that God and man no longer had to be separated. **Matthew 27:51** It also displayed the truth that only God could tear down the barrier between God and man. The *Ark of the Covenant* represented the presence of God. The *mercy seat* represented His mercy.

According to **Hebrews 10:3-4,** none of these sacrifices ever paid for people's sin. Since an animal is not equal to a human, an animal's death is not equal to a human's death. Thus, an animal's death can never fully pay for a person's sin. The purpose of the sacrificing of animals was to continually remind the people of their sin and it's punishment. It was also to cause a yearning for the future Deliverer, the Lamb of God, who would die to take away the sins of all people. Since in God's mind, Christ had already died for the sins of the world, God applied the death of Christ to those who came to Him in faith, recognizing their sin and trusting in God's mercy to forgive them. **Revelation 13:8**

Certainly, any intimacy one felt with God would be limited because the people were separated from God. The people might have realized God's love and faithfulness to them, but their intimacy with Him had to be limited.

Today a relationship with God would be more revealing because there is no separation between saved man and Father. In **Romans 8:14-17** we read *"For all who are being led by the Spirit of God, these are sons of God. For you have not received a spirit of slavery leading to fear again, but you have received a spirit of adoption as sons by which we cry out, 'Abba! Father!' The Spirit Himself testifies with our spirit that we are children of God, and if children, heirs also, heirs of God and fellow heirs with Christ, if indeed we suffer with Him so that we may also be glorified with Him."* Abba is like saying "Daddy."

Today, believers can come to Him freely, with confidence. We are fully assured that our sin has been paid for and that He sees us as holy. We are welcomed and urged to approach God boldly, as His children. He desires us to come to Him in any and all circumstances. He tells us blatantly to come to Him when we are in need in this passage. We don't have to get our life together to come to Him. He wants us to come in our need and allow Him to be God there.

SUMMARY

- God is loving, merciful and gracious.

- Unsaved man is a sinner and cannot make himself acceptable to God.

- Man can come to God only according to God's will and plan.

- Man cannot be in God's presence unless he is holy, that is, without sin.

FOR CONSIDERATION

Allow God to remind you that He is your Life this week by reflecting upon His holiness and His grace in making a way for sinful mankind to be in His presence.

CHAPTER 9
Israel's History

Numbers 13:1-14:35; Joshua 1:1-5;11:23; 24:19-24;
Judges 2:8-19; 1Samuel 8:4-9; 9:15-17;
2Samuel 5:3-5; 7:4-16; 1Kings 2:1-12;
2Kings 16:1-4; 17:1-6; 25:8-12; Malachi 3:6-7;
John 10:10; Romans 6:11-14; 7:4-13;
1Corinthians 15:55-58;
Galatians 2:1-5; 2:19-21: Hebrews 13:7-9;
James 1:16-18; 2Peter 1:3; 3:8-10

This chapter covers several hundred years-~1500BC-
~600BC-in the historical books **Numbers** through
2Chronicles. You will learn a basic overview of the
history of Israel.

In the last chapter, Israel was still around Mt. Sinai and
had just finished the Tabernacle. They continued on in
their journey towards Canaan, the land God had
promised to them through Abraham. However, they did
not conquer the land because of lack of faith and God
punished them to forty years of wandering in the desert.
During their wanderings, they complained constantly.
This takes place in the **Book of Numbers**. Forty years
later, the old generation had died and the new generation
was ready to enter the land. Moses then reviewed all the
details of the Law with the people. They again
responded with *"we will obey"*. Moses died and Joshua
was appointed to lead the Israelites into Canaan. This
takes place in the **Book of Deuteronomy**.

Through God's leading and under Joshua, the Israelites
conquered the land of Canaan. Their first victory
involved the fall of Jericho. They then divided the land
into 12 areas - one for each of the 12 Tribes of Israel -

and settled into the land. God's promise had been fulfilled. God had commanded the Israelites to completely destroy all of the Canaanites in order to remove the pagan influence from the land. However, the Israelites disobeyed and the evil religious practices of the Canaanites would later entice the Israelites away from total allegiance to God. This is seen in the **Book of Joshua**.

From this point on, the purity of the Israelites and their obedience to God and His Law degenerated. They worshipped idols and rebelled against God. Since God's blessings or curses depended upon their obedience to the Law, when they rebelled, God would allow other nations to defeat and oppress the Israelites. The Israelites would then cry out to God and He would graciously raise up a leader or judge to deliver them.

After a while, they would turn away from God again. The cycle repeated itself for a total of seven times. This is recorded in the Book of Judges. The sin of the Israelites showed that they had a sinful nature and were under Satan's influence. Their hearts were selfish and evil. However, every time the people turned to God, He would graciously provide deliverance and blessing. God's extravagant mercy far overshadows the sins of Israel.

The Israelites became dissatisfied having God as their King and wanted a human king like the other nations. This was the ultimate rejection of God as their leader. God granted them their wish and Saul became the first of many kings of Israel. Saul eventually turned from God's ways and God appointed David to be king around the year 1000BC. This is recorded in the Book of 1Samuel.

David was "a man after God's heart", but he stumbled and sinned greatly against God. Still, because he acknowledged his sin and turned to God, He forgave David and used him mightily. David wrote many of the **Psalms** and established Israel's dominance in the land. This is recorded in **2Samuel** and **1Chronicles**. God also promised to send the coming Deliverer through David's family line. This promise is called the *Davidic Covenant.* The future Deliverer was referred to as the "Son of David". David's son Solomon was the next king. He was given tremendous wisdom, which he used to write many **Proverbs**, plus the **Books of Ecclesiastes** and **Song of Solomon**. God used Solomon to build a magnificent permanent temple, which was similar in design to the portable Tabernacle. However, Solomon also disobeyed God in many ways, which are recorded in **1Kings** and **2Chronicles**.

After Solomon's death, the nation of Israel broke off into two opposing nations. The Northern Kingdom was called Israel and the Southern Kingdom was named Judah. Other than for occasional exceptions by some of the kings of Judah, both kingdoms rebelled against God and His Laws and worshipped other gods.

Sin in the land reached a new *high. (Signifying amount of sin increased)*. Some of the Israelites even went to the point of sacrificing their own children and practicing divination and sorcery. God sent many prophets, such as Isaiah, Jeremiah and Hosea to warn the nations of God's coming judgment. God would surely punish their sin. However, God promised to forgive all of the people's sins if they simply acknowledged their sin and turned back to Him. This is called "repentance." It is a 180° turn in the opposite direction. Instead of turning from God, they would turn back to Him. They would be in relationship with Him as their God and Father. From

Genesis to Revelation, God has always been willing to forgive because it is Who He is. This is also seen in the New Testament:

"But do not let this one fact escape your notice, beloved, that with the Lord one day is like a thousand years, and a thousand years like one day. The Lord is not slow about His promise, as some count slowness, but is patient toward you, not wishing for any to perish but for all to come to repentance. But the day of the Lord will come like a thief, in which the heavens will pass away with a roar and the elements will be destroyed with intense heat, and the earth and its works will be burned up." **2Peter 3:8-10**

Still, the people rejected God and His prophets. So God sent other nations to conquer them. In 722BC, the nation of Assyria conquered the Northern Kingdom of Israel and took many people captive. In 586BC, the Babylonians conquered the Southern Kingdom of Judah and destroyed Jerusalem and the temple. They carried off many of the Israelites into exile into Babylon. This takes place in **2Kings** and **2Chronicles**.

The curses, which God had warned of many years before in **Deuteronomy 28**, had now fallen upon the Israelites. The nation of Israel no longer existed. Its people were scattered everywhere. Jerusalem lay in ruins. The temple was destroyed. Had God forgotten His people? What was to come of God's plans to send a Deliverer? The next chapter will show that, even though Israel rejected God, He was still faithful to His people and His promises. Isn't it wonderful to know that in this day and age, from the very beginning of creation, that there is someone you can fully count on? Someone who will *never* let you down? Someone who is the same yesterday, today and forever?

" 'For I, the LORD, do not change; therefore you, O sons of Jacob, are not consumed. From the days of your fathers you have turned aside from My statutes and have not kept them. Return to Me, and I will return to you,' says the LORD of hosts. 'But you say, 'How shall we return?' " **Malachi 3:6-7**

"Do not be deceived, my beloved brethren. Every good thing given and every perfect gift is from above, coming down from the Father of lights, with whom there is no variation or shifting shadow. In the exercise of His will He brought us forth by the word of truth, so that we would be a kind of first fruits among His creatures."
James 1:16-18

"Remember those who led you, who spoke the word of God to you; and considering the result of their conduct, imitate their faith. Jesus Christ is the same yesterday and today and forever. Do not be carried away by varied and strange teachings; for it is good for the heart to be strengthened by grace, not by foods, through which those who were so occupied were not benefited."
Hebrews 13:7-9

Lasting fruit did not come from God's exhortations to obey because unsaved man is sinful. The root of Israel's disobedience was a sinful, evil heart. They inherited a sin nature from Adam and their selfish actions proved it.

The New Testament verses **Romans 6:11-14** and **1Corinthians 15:56-57** reveal that the Law actually brings about disobedience, not obedience. An analogy to the Law is a sign that says "Stay Off The Grass" or

"No Fishing Allowed". Usually, when we read a sign like that, we feel an urge to do the opposite. We are tempted whether it is from the flesh, Satan or the world system. This urge is actually brought on by the suggestion of the sign. The same is true with the Old Testament Law or Ten Commandments. **Romans 7:4-13**. The Law or Old Covenant did nothing to change someone's heart. In fact, the more the people were exhorted to obey them, the more they disobeyed. Even the warnings of destruction and exile did little to inhibit their selfish, rebellious lifestyle.

As discussed in chapter seven, the main purpose of the Ten Commandments was actually to point out people's sin so that they would turn to God for mercy and look forward to the coming Deliverer. That is why simply exhorting people to obey God doesn't produce lasting fruit, both back then and today. The reason is "the power of sin is in the Law" **1Corinthians 15:56.** God's way to produce obedience in our lives is first through a thorough understanding of His grace. That is why Paul says the reason that sin will not be our master is because we are not under Law, but under grace. **Romans 6:14**

Thus the Old Testament shows man's sinful nature and desperate need for a cure. Man needs radical heart surgery. Simply telling people what to obey will not produce true lasting fruit. The Old Testament proves it. God's answer through Christ was to provide a radical heart surgery by making believers into new creations and by placing in them Himself who is the ability to follow God.

In **Galatians 2:1-5** it says that our old, sinful nature is crucified with Christ at the cross; In **Romans 6** they are indwelt by the very life of Christ Himself. In **Romans 8** this provides the desire and means to obey God. That means to obey God is Jesus living through us. He is the only one who is able to live the Christian Life. Through an understanding of what God in His grace has done at the cross and His continued grace in our lives, Christians are able to follow Him in a love relationship. **Galatians 2:19-21** Because Christ lives in us, we are able to live the Christian Life. We rest from trying to do it in our own power and allow Christ to live His Life through us. All of this is God's wonderful provision to believers through His grace. Jesus talks about the Christian Life as having life and life abundantly.

"The thief comes only to steal and kill and destroy; I came that they may have life, and have it abundantly." **John 10:10**

Saved persons have everything they need in order to live this abundant life. They have Jesus living in them and through them. *"seeing that His divine power has granted to us everything pertaining to life and godliness, through the true knowledge of Him who called us by His own glory and excellence."* **2Peter 1:3**

God was faithful to respond to Israel whenever they turned to Him for forgiveness and help. He was also faithful to pronounce curses upon them in accordance with the Mosaic Covenant. **Deuteronomy 28**

God punished Israel for their disobedience, sometimes through death. When David committed adultery, he knew that he deserved to die as punishment for his sin. When Solomon dedicated the temple, several thousand animals were sacrificed. These sacrifices were a reminder that God demands death as the penalty for sin. God continued to be patient with His people. He brought them into the land, rose up judges to deliver them, gave them kings upon their request and continually warned them of the coming judgment. He gave them opportunities again and again to turn back to Him. When David sinned with Bathsheba, he acknowledged his sin and God graciously forgave him. Even in judgment, God never forsook His people.

Israel's constant sinful attitude and actions revealed their sin nature. They were descendants of Adam. They were born sinners and they were in slavery to Satan and to sin. They did not and could not fully obey God's Law because their heart was sinful. They were helpless to save themselves. They desperately needed God's mercy and grace.

It was God who set the terms of the Mosaic Covenant. Israel would be blessed by total obedience to the Law. Man could not come to God in his own way and be accepted by God. He could not do whatever he wanted and receive God's blessings. This is dramatically seen in David's life when he sinned against God. David could not reverse his sin or its consequences. He was guilty before God. But God forgave him because David acknowledged his sin and came to God for forgiveness. He trusted in God's provision of grace. It was David's faith in God, not his actions that brought cleansing.

God's faithfulness is seen in the life of David. Not only was David forgiven of adultery, but also murder! Not just only in David's life but with all of Israel! Time after time they chased after other gods - which weren't gods at all! Time after time Father pursued them to have as His own.

God wanted to bless Israel and give her His best. He continually forgave Israel and patiently waited for her to turn back to Him. Israel's punishment came after repeated warnings and pleadings from God and His messengers. Father was so patient with them and us. If you view God as one who is waiting to punish every sin, you have a false view of God, which could inhibit you from experiencing His love and grace. Father always disciplines us in love so we might understand how destructive sin is in our life and how much He always wants the best for His children, even if that means they must temporarily suffer in order to see more clearly.

"and you have forgotten the exhortation which is addressed to you as sons, "My son, do not regard lightly the discipline of the Lord, Nor faint when you are reproved by Him; For those whom the Lord loves He disciplines, And He scourges every son whom He receives. It is for discipline that you endure; God deals with you as with sons; for what son is there whom his father does not discipline? But if you are without discipline, of which all have become partakers, then you are illegitimate children and not sons. Furthermore, we had earthly fathers to discipline us, and we respected them; shall we not much rather be subject to the Father of spirits, and live? For they disciplined us for a short time as seemed best to them, but He disciplines us for our good, so that we may share His holiness. All discipline for the moment seems not to be joyful, but sorrowful; yet to those who have been trained by it, afterwards it yields the peaceful fruit of righteousness."
Hebrews 12:5-11

SUMMARY

- God is faithful.

- God is holy, righteous and demands death as the penalty for sin.

- God is loving, merciful and gracious.

- Unsaved man *is* a sinner and cannot make himself acceptable to God.

- Man can come to God only according to God's will and plan.

- Man must have faith in order to please God and be saved.

- The only way to please God is to trust that God is living His life through you in the Person of Jesus Christ. Nothing less than perfection is acceptable to God. Only Jesus has lived or can live the perfect life!

FOR CONSIDERATION

Allow God to remind you that He is your Life this week by reflecting upon His patience and faithfulness to you.

CHAPTER 10
God's Prophets

Isaiah 7:14; 9:6-7; 52:13 - 53:12;
Jeremiah 3:12-14; 5:1; 9:13-16; 11:6-14a; 15:19-20;
Jeremiah 31:20; 31:31-34; Ezekiel 36:16-38;
Micah 5:2; Matthew 9:36; 11:20-30; 23:25-39;
Mark 2:1-12; 6:30-56; Luke 1:1-5:11; 7:11-17;
John 1:1-34; 3:17; 3:21; 6:28-29; 10:8-39; 14:6;
John 15:1-8; 16:5-15;
1Peter 2:22: Revelation 19:11-16

At the end of the previous story, the Israelites were exiled to Babylon and the temple and city of Jerusalem were destroyed. God had repeatedly sent prophets to warn the people of punishment if they did not turn back to Him. The people rejected the prophets and followed the desires of their own hearts. They were sinners under the influence of Satan and they refused to come to God for healing.

Even after they continue to reject God, He offered complete forgiveness if they would only admit their sin *(agree with God that what they did was wrong)* and turn to Him *(repent - going in the opposite direction away from the sin)* for healing. But the threat of punishment and exile did not deter the Israelites from their sinful ways. Their hearts were hardened with unbelief about their sin, God's threat of punishment and their need for forgiveness and a Deliverer.

Now, with Israel no longer a nation, but living in exile, what was to come of God's covenant with His people and His plans to send a Deliverer? God used many prophets to reassure the people that He had not forgotten them. The prophets had not only warned the people of

God's judgment, they also encouraged the people that God would again return them to Jerusalem after 70 years of exile in Babylon.

Jeremiah spoke of a New Covenant that God would make with His people. It would not be like the Mosaic Covenant. This was a written code that merely revealed the people's sin and condemned them. Instead, God said, *"...I will put My law within them and on their heart I will write it; and I will be their God, and they shall be My people. For I will forgive their iniquity, and their sin I will remember no more."* **Jeremiah 31:33-34**

This time, God would come and be the Keeper of the covenant within His people. How can we follow God? What do we have to do?

"Jesus answered and said to them, 'This is the work of God, that you believe in Him whom He has sent.'" **John 6:29**

"Moreover, I will give you a new heart and put a new spirit within you; and I will remove the heart of stone from your flesh and give you a heart of flesh. I will put My Spirit within you and cause you to walk in My statutes, and you will be careful to observe My ordinances." **Ezekiel 36:26-27**

To believe in Jesus is all that is required in order to be saved. He puts a new heart in us. He exchanges our hard heart for a flesh heart, a tender heart. He puts a new spirit in us. He also puts His own Spirit in us - the Holy Spirit. He does everything in this covenant. He also causes us to believe and to have faith in Jesus. He has given each of us "a measure of faith!" That "measure of faith" is revealed in us through all of life's circumstances that we encounter. Father reveals that faith in us through our entire earthly existence. The believer is one who lives by faith - there is no other way.

"³ For through the grace given to me I say to everyone among you not to think more highly of himself than he ought to think; but to think so as to have sound judgment, as God has allotted to each a measure of faith." **Romans 12:3**

God initiates our salvation; He sustains it and He perfects it through His Son living in us and through us. Jesus is our Life. There is no other Life to live.

Many prophets spoke of the coming Deliverer. Their prophecies included the following. He would be born in Bethlehem, of a virgin; He would be born in the family line of David. He would suffer for the sins of many.

A small percentage of Israelites, called *a remnant*, began to return to Jerusalem in 538BC. This took place when God opened the heart of the king of Persia, who allowed them to return to their land. Over the next 100 years, the Jewish people rebuilt the temple, the city of Jerusalem and began worshipping God again. Although they did not return to idol worship, their hearts once again turned cold towards God. God's final prophet of the Old Testament, Malachi, spoke around the year 400BC and rebuked religious hypocrisy. Starting with the priests, the Israelites did not honor God. When they needed something, they'd call on Him. When they weren't in need, they'd ignore Him. They definitely did not give their best to Him in any area of their lives.

"A son honors his father, and a servant his master. Then if I am a Father, where is My honor? And if I am a Master, where is My respect?' says the LORD of hosts to you, 'O priests who despise My name. But you say, 'How

have we despised Your name? You are presenting defiled food upon My altar? But you say, 'How have we defiled You?' In that you say, 'The table of the LORD is to be despised.' But when you present the blind for sacrifice, is it not evil? And when you present the lame and sick, is it not evil? Why not offer it to your governor? Would he be pleased with you? Or would he receive you kindly? says the LORD of hosts. But now will you not entreat God's favor, that He may be gracious to us? With such an offering on your part, will He receive any of you kindly?' says the LORD of hosts. Oh that there were one among you who would shut the gates, that you might not uselessly kindle fire on My altar! I am not pleased with you,' says the LORD of hosts, 'nor will I accept an offering from you. For from the rising of the sun even to its setting, My name will be great among the nations, and in every place incense is going to be offered to My name, and a grain offering that is pure; for My name will be great among the nations,' says the LORD of hosts. But you are profaning it, in that you say, 'The table of the Lord is defiled, and as for its fruit, its food is to be despised.' You also say, My, how tiresome it is! And you disdainfully sniff at it, says the LORD of hosts, and you bring what was taken by robbery and what is lame or sick; so you bring the offering! Should I receive that from your hand? says the LORD. But cursed be the swindler who has a male in his flock and vows it, but sacrifices a blemished animal to the Lord, for I am a great King, says the LORD of hosts, and My name is feared among the nation." **Malachi 1:6-14**

For the next 400 years, God remained silent. There were neither prophets nor divinely inspired writings. During this time, the Jewish people lived under the rule of other powers. First, the Greeks gained control of the land and then the Romans. Many Jewish people waited anxiously for the coming of the promised Deliverer. They looked for a King who would come and defeat the Romans and rule over their land. They were expecting a conquering King to physically remove the Romans. Little did they know they had a deeper problem - a spiritual one! They needed their sins forgiven and to know how to depend on God to live His Life through them. But it had been 400 years since God had spoken. Had God forgotten His promises through the prophets? Under the oppression of the Romans, the Jewish people waited with great expectancy for their King who would deliver them.

God created people so they could know how great His love is for them. He wanted them to love Him in return and have fellowship with Him forever. However, man's sin broke this relationship between God and man. Sin separated man from God and transferred man from God's family to Satan's family. In God's love, mercy and grace, He desired to reconcile man back to Himself.

God is also just and man's sin had to be punished by eternal death. So God devised a plan in which He would send a Deliverer who would take man's punishment for sin upon Himself and die to pay the penalty of all man's sin. The Savior would satisfy God's justice and restore man back to God. Throughout the Old Testament, God had prepared the world for this Deliverer. He also prepared a people, the nation of Israel, through whom the Deliverer would come. The sacrificing of animals by the Israelites as a substitute for their sin pictured what the Deliverer would do for people.

This Savior was to reconcile man to God. This Savior needed to be more than man if His death was to be sufficient to pay for all people's sins. He also needed to be sinless in order to fulfill God's standard of holiness as an unblemished sacrifice. Yet, to be the Deliverer of all people, He needed to identify with them in some way. The only one who could possibly meet these requirements was one who was both fully God and fully man. God, who is One, has always existed as three persons: God the Father, God the Son and God the Holy Spirit. The second person of the *Trinity,* God the Son, was the one who came to earth and took on human form in order to become mankind's Deliverer. God not only cared enough to send a Deliverer, He Himself would be the Deliverer in Jesus Christ. Then, humanly speaking, God does what no one would ever expect: He visits the planet Himself in the Person of Jesus Christ.

Despite the people's constant rebellion against Him, God persisted in reminding them through His prophets of His promise to send a Deliverer to them. God was faithful to His promise to punish disobedience to the Mosaic Covenant. He was also faithful to the Abrahamic Covenant in which He promised never to forget His people, regardless of their actions.

God warned the Israelites that He would punish them if they refused to turn to Him to be healed. Because of their sin, many of them died through the hands of the Assyrians and Babylonians. God lovingly tried to bring Israel back to Him. He gave them countless opportunities to simply admit their sin, turn to Him and allow Him to heal them. In His mercy, He withheld judgment for many years. However, because He is fair, just and holy, He had to judge the people according to the conditions of the Mosaic Covenant, which the people had agreed to and promised to abide by.

However, even in judgment, He withheld the full punishment of death upon the Israelites. In His grace, He promised them a return to their land and future blessings. He promised a New Covenant and to give them a new heart and spirit. He promised a Deliverer. All of these things He promised to Israel while they were in the midst of complete rebellion and rejection of God. God was loving, merciful and gracious to His people because of who He is, not because of their actions towards Him.

Man was living in spiritual darkness and in slavery to Satan. His heart was sinful, selfish and in rebellion towards God. He even rejected God's offer of forgiveness. Since God is holy and perfect, there is no way that man can enter into His presence through his own efforts. **Isaiah 6:1-7**

It was God who set the terms of the Mosaic Covenant. Israel would be blessed by total obedience to the Law. Man could not come to God in his own way and be accepted by God, although Israel did try to do this. They still maintained their religious practices during the time period of this chapter. But they were attempting to come to God according to their own will and plan, not God's.

They worshipped other gods and engaged in all kinds of sinful behavior. They refused to worship only the Lord and to follow His ways. Even when they continued their sacrifices and rituals, they were merely external and religious; they did not come from a heart of repentance and dependence. They had no relationship with God. God therefore rejected their attempts to approach Him in this way.

God accepted and forgave His people through their faith in Him. God's plan at this point was to show people their need for a substitute through the picture of animals regularly being sacrificed. The heart condition that God required was simply one of belief in one's sinfulness before God and helplessness to make oneself acceptable to Him. God did not require them to "clean up their hearts" before they could come to Him. It was God Who did the cleansing. Israel only needed to admit their sin and turn to God for healing. But in their pride, they rejected God's truth while still maintaining their religious rituals.

External religiosity has been around since the day Adam and Eve tried to cover their nakedness with their own covering of fig leaves. Today, people try to cover their sin with their own covering of fig leaves. Today, people go through religious rituals to try to please God. Because God is holy and perfect, He will always reject people's efforts to make themselves acceptable to Him. This principle also holds true for Christians today.

Their daily acceptance by God is based upon their perfect standing in Christ, not their own daily performance. To try to make ourselves acceptable to God negates the work of Jesus on the cross. God will reject Christians' efforts to present themselves as acceptable to Him based upon their performance. God's acceptance of them is complete and always based upon the righteousness they were given through faith. **Romans 3:21-22** Man must realize the truth of his sin and that God and God alone has the means of making sinful man acceptable to Him. He offers this freely to all who come to Him according to His will and plan.

The heart condition that God required was simply one of belief in one's sinfulness before God and helplessness to make one's self-acceptable to Him. With this realization of sin, the people needed to look to God for His rescue plan and Deliverer.

Both were initiated by God and involved following God's ways. The Old Covenant involved blessings and curses, depending on one's total obedience to God's commands. **Deuteronomy 28** It was a continual reminder to the people of their sins, shortcomings and God's holiness. Day after day, it revealed people's sins and need for forgiveness. Day after day, the Old Covenant proclaimed punishment for disobedience. But nothing in the Old Covenant could change someone's heart. It was purely an external system of moral laws and left man's sinful heart untouched.

In contrast, the New Covenant is a wonderful improvement over the Old. God said that He would put His law on their hearts and minds. **Jeremiah 31:31-34** What does this mean? With the help of other Scripture, mainly from the New Testament, we now have a clearer picture of what God was saying. The Old Covenant could not renew man's sinful core, since man's problem was a sinful heart because he was born in Adam. Therefore, God promised to renew man by renewing his heart and placing His commands on man's heart. Those who place their trust in the Deliverer would become a new creation. **2Corinthians 5:17** They would become people with a new heart and God's Spirit living in them. **Ezekiel 36:25-28** God would even place in His children, the desire and ability to obey Him. **Philippians 2:13**

Before Adam and Eve sinned, they were perfect - without sin. Their hearts were pure and their spirits alive. God had breathed into them the breath of life. In other words, God's own Spirit lived in them, something that was not true of the animals. Adam and Eve were spiritually alive and living in union with God. When they sinned, all of this changed. They became spiritually dead. They were now under the influence of Satan rather than God. Their hearts were selfish and darkened by sin. They could no longer   discern truth from lies. They were no longer in union with God. From this point on, the remainder of the Old Testament shows the out-workings of man's sinful heart and spiritual deadness.

God promised to give people a new heart and a new spirit - God's own Spirit. Their relationship would change towards God. They would now have a relationship with Him. Their heart would change from being an enemy of God to being a friend. They would be taken from death to life. They would change from a heart of disobedience to a heart of obedience because God Himself would give them the desire to follow Him. Jesus would live His Life through them as they rested in the finished work of Jesus. All that Jesus did was credited to saved individuals. The only thing they would need to do is to believe. And even that He gave them the heart and faith to do!

One should be able to see from the readings that God's desire is to renew and restore fallen man. Only as a last resort, after repeated warnings, did God take disciplinary action on His people. Even then, His purpose was to restore them. If God desired to punish us, we would have no hope and He never would have sent His only Son to suffer and die for us. If He desired to punish us, we would have all been separated from God in hell a long time ago. It's important to understand God's true heart before we can really experience His love and enjoy a relationship with Him.

SUMMARY

- God promises a future Deliverer as told by his through the prophets.

- God is faithful.

- God is holy, righteous and demands death as the penalty for sin.

- God is loving, merciful and gracious.

- Unsaved man is a sinner and cannot make himself acceptable to God.

- Man can come to God only according to God's will and plan.

- Man must have faith in order to please God and be saved.

- The only way to please God is to trust that God is living His Life through you.

- Nothing less than perfection is acceptable to God.

- He is our Perfect Life, our only Life.

FOR CONSIDERATION

Allow God to remind you that He is your Life this week by reflecting on His faithfulness to you, even when you can't hear Him. You may be lonely at times, but you're never alone. Also, consider His heart to restore and renew you. Sit before Him silently and allow Him to speak to you.

CHAPTER 11
The Deliverer's Birth & Life

Matthew 9:36; 11:20-30; 23:25-39;
Mark 2:1-12; 6:30-56; Luke 1:1 - 5:11; 7:11-17;
John 1:1-34; 3:17; 6:28-29; 10:8-39; 14:6; 15:1-8;
John 16:5-15; 1Peter 2:22; Revelation 19:11-16

"Have this attitude in yourselves which was also in Christ Jesus, who, although He existed in the form of God, did not regard equality with God a thing to be grasped, but emptied Himself, taking the form of a bond-servant, and being made in the likeness of men. Being found in appearance as a man, He humbled Himself by becoming obedient to the point of death, even death on a cross." **Philippians 2:5-8**

THE COMING OF THE DELIVERER

The year was around 3-5BC. The Jewish people lived under the rule of the Roman Empire and were waiting expectantly for the coming of their Deliverer. A young virgin named Mary, who was engaged to be married to Joseph, received a vision that she was to miraculously give birth to a son. His name would be Jesus, which means Savior. He would be called the Son of God. To be the Son of anything is to say that I resemble my parents. In this case, the Son of God would resemble His Father - God. Jesus is also called the son of man. He resembled His human

Mother - human. Jesus was born one night in a stable in Bethlehem as the prophets had predicted. From the onset, Jesus was born into rejection. Although the King of kings and the Lord of lords, He had no prestigious place for His birth. **Revelation 19:11-16 & John 1:1-**

5,14 The Creator of everything and everyone was born in a stable! That He would come to this earth as a baby, let alone a human being, was condescending. *"who, although He existed in the form of God, did not regard equality with God a thing to be grasped, but emptied Himself, taking the form of a bond-servant, and being made in the likeness of men."* **Philippians 2:6-7**

Farm animals were His companions at birth. This is God we are talking about! Yet, He would take on human form as Jesus in order to identify with and save His creation from eternal punishment in hell. God the Son had entered the world both fully God and fully man. Because He was born of the Holy Spirit, Jesus was not born a sinner like all humans, quite the contrary; He had no sin in Him.

A prophet named John the Baptist was preparing the people for the Deliverer by calling all people to repent and be baptized. One day, when Jesus was about 30 years old, He appeared at the place where John was baptizing. John exclaimed, *"Behold, the Lamb of God, who takes away the sin of the world!"* **John 1:29** Jesus told John to baptize Him.

"Then Jesus arrived from Galilee at the Jordan coming to John, to be baptized by him. But John tried to prevent Him, saying, 'I have need to be baptized by You, and do You come to me?' But Jesus answering said to him, 'Permit it at this time; for in this way it is fitting for us to fulfill all righteousness.' Then he permitted Him." **Matthew 3:13-15**

In the next verse we read these staggering words. Then Jesus began His public ministry. Father wanted to show everyone present at the baptism, as well as you and I today, that He loves and accepts us not based on our

performance.   Jesus had not officially begun His
ministry at the time of His baptism. Now we can go out
in life knowing the difference between performance
based acceptance and acceptance based performance
with our Father.

After this, Jesus went into the desert and fasted for forty
days. Satan knew that Jesus was God's Deliverer and he
wanted to stop God's rescue plan for man.   Satan tried
to tempt Jesus by offering Him all the kingdoms of the
world if He would fall down and worship him. Unlike
all humans, Jesus resisted Satan and overcame him, thus
showing Himself to be more powerful than Satan.

Jesus then began His public ministry in Israel as God's
Deliverer. He taught that He was not only God's Son
but that He was equal to God and that salvation came
through Him alone. *"Jesus said to him, 'I am the way,
and the truth, and the life; no one comes to the Father
but through Me.'"* **John 14:6**   He said that He came not
to condemn the world, but to save the world through
Him.   When asked; *"'what must we do to do the works
God requires?'"*   **John 3:17** *"Jesus answered and said
to them, 'This is the work of God, that you believe in
Him whom He has sent.'"* **John 6:29** Those who did not
believe stood condemned already because of their sin.
They were condemned to eternal punishment in hell.

He also said that He was the way, the truth, the life, the
light of the world and the good shepherd. In **Matthew
11:28-30,** Jesus said, *"Come to Me, all who are weary
and heavy-laden, and I will give you rest. Take My yoke
upon you and learn from Me, for I am gentle and humble
in heart, and YOU WILL FIND REST FOR YOUR SOULS. For
My yoke is easy and My burden is light."* The rest that
Jesus was offering was a permanent state of rest for our
tumultuous souls.   Our souls are comprised of mind,

emotions and will. He gave us the ability to think, to feel and to choose. The burden would now be light indeed!

Jesus would live His Life through us. What was our job? To believe Him! The ability to believe was even given to us by Him! Jesus knew that all people were sinful, lost and in slavery to Satan. He had compassion on them, *"Seeing the people, He felt compassion for them, because they were distressed and dispirited like sheep without a shepherd."* **Matthew 9:36**

Jesus proved He was God by performing many miracles. He showed His power over Satan by casting demons out of people. He showed His power over nature by calming a storm, walking on water and multiplying loaves of bread and fish. He showed His power over sickness and death by healing many and raising several people from the dead. He had power to forgive sins, something, which only God could do. **Mark 2:1-12**

Like today, many in that time did not realize the depth of their need for Jesus. The blind were healed but those who had their sight were blinded by their sin. The cripple would walk, but those who could walk were crippled by their attitudes. The deaf were healed but those who could hear were deaf to God's call to them. Not only did Jesus heal many, Jesus Himself committed no sin in His lifetime. **1Peter 2:22**

Initially, Jesus was very popular, as many people believed that He was God's Deliverer. However, they expected a military and political leader who would free them from bondage to Rome. When Jesus told them that His kingdom was spiritual, many stopped following Him. The Pharisees, Sadducees and Scribes, who were Jewish religious leaders, strongly opposed Jesus because

He exposed their evil hearts. He called them hypocrites and told them that they would be punished in hell. He said this that they might acknowledge their sin and turn to Him to be forgiven. Instead, the religious leaders continued in their self-righteousness and plotted to silence Him by killing Him.

Jesus had 12 disciples who followed Him closely. Near the end of His 3 1/2 years of ministry, Jesus told His disciples that He must go to Jerusalem, where He would suffer, die and then rise again. The disciples did not understand why this was to happen. Knowing the agony that lay ahead of Him, yet desiring to fulfill His purpose as the Savior of the world, Jesus headed toward Jerusalem during the time of the Jewish Passover feast.

"Jesus said to him, 'I am the way, and the truth, and the life; no one comes to the Father but through Me.'" **John 14:6**

Jesus was initially popular with many of the Jews who were interested in a military/political king who would lead them to freedom from the Romans. Jesus knew their motives and refused to accept such a role. Instead, He spoke of spiritual matters. This caused many to stop following Him. These people were also more interested in seeing miracles than in hearing God's truth about their sin.

Jesus was even more unpopular with another group - the religious leaders. Jesus was a   threat to their authority and position. They were self-righteous and blind to their sin and hypocrisy. Despite witnessing some of Jesus' miracles, they would not recognize Him as the Deliverer. Instead, they plotted to kill Him. It was to this latter group, namely the Pharisees, Sadducees and Scribes, that Jesus reserved His harshest words:

"Woe to you, scribes and Pharisees, hypocrites! For you clean the outside of the cup and of the dish, but inside they are full of robbery and self-indulgence. You blind Pharisee, first clean the inside of the cup and of the dish, so that the outside of it may become clean also. Woe to you, scribes and Pharisees, hypocrites! For you are like whitewashed tombs, which on the outside appear beautiful, but inside they are full of dead men's bones and all uncleanness. So you, too, outwardly appear righteous to men, but inwardly you are full of hypocrisy and lawlessness. Woe to you, scribes and Pharisees, hypocrites! For you build the tombs of the prophets and adorn the monuments of the righteous, and say, 'If we had been living in the days of our fathers, we would not have been partners with them in shedding the blood of the prophets.' So you testify against yourselves, that you are sons of those who murdered the prophets. Fill up, then, the measure of the guilt of your fathers. You serpents, you brood of vipers, how will you escape the sentence of hell? Therefore, behold, I am sending you prophets and wise men and scribes; some of them you will kill and crucify, and some of them you will scourge in your synagogues, and persecute from city to city, so that upon you may fall the guilt of all the righteous blood shed on earth, from the blood of righteous Abel to the blood of Zechariah, the son of Berechiah, whom you murdered between the temple and the altar. Truly I say to you, all these things will come upon this generation. Jerusalem, Jerusalem, who kills the prophets and stones those who are sent to her! How often I wanted to gather your children together, the way a hen gathers her chicks under her wings, and you were unwilling. Behold, your house is being left to you desolate! For I say to you, from now on you will not see Me until you say, 'Blessed is He who comes in the name of the Lord!" **Matthew 23:25-39**

Jesus was popular with those who recognized their need for Him. Prostitutes, tax collectors, lepers, the sick and outcasts often received Him and His words. Jesus was never shocked by man's sin. In fact, John declares that Jesus *"for He knew all men."* **John 2:24-25** Jesus knew that He could forgive any sin, no matter how great. All that was required was for someone to recognize their sin and come to Him for healing and forgiveness.

Many expected a military/political leader. So they would have expected a physically strong, warrior-type leader. Instead, Jesus was gentle, humble, meek and compassionate. In fact, it was the first time that God was ever described as humble. Humble was always used as a negative term to describe someone in literature up to this point in history. Humble usually meant a poor, undesirable, nobody that no one would want to be around or have around them. He described Himself as the Good Shepherd.

He was a servant. He was totally dependent on His Father. He was loving, merciful and gracious. Many were looking for the wrong type of leader. Like most people, they believed that life would be better if only the circumstances changed. They wanted a leader to give them a different circumstance, from being ruled over, to self-rule. To be in control! They didn't realize that their real need was that of life exchange - His for theirs!

No matter what circumstance they found themselves in, they were still dead in their sins and a slave to Satan. They needed life but not just any other life! They needed a relationship with their Creator. They needed Jesus as their Life, their only Life! We don't realize that our biggest problem is us not our circumstance. Jesus came to give us a new heart, make us a new creation. He came to exchange our dead life for His. He didn't come to change our conditions but our "condition." Allowing Him to live through us, we could soar over the circumstances. We could rest in Him knowing that though it may not look or feel like it at times, He was in complete control! We need not worry.

In **Matthew 6:14-15** we read *"For if you forgive others for their transgressions, your heavenly Father will also forgive you. But if you do not forgive others, then your Father will not forgive your transgressions'"* Is there anyone in your life that you need to forgive, including yourself? If so, who?

Hopefully, people will see Jesus' heart to forgive and restore mankind. Take some time and if a few feel free to share, allow them to. They don't have to go into graphic details. Encourage the group to silently pray for awhile and ask Father who, if anyone, from their past that they may need to apologize and ask forgiveness to. Encourage them to pray for that person and trust that whatever forgiveness is to be had has already been taken care of by Father.

SUMMARY

- Jesus is God's Son and is equal to God.

- Jesus has power over Satan, nature, sickness and death.

- Jesus is the Lamb of God, God's Deliverer.

- Jesus is perfect - without sin.

- Jesus can forgive sins and give people eternal life.

- Unsaved man is a sinner and cannot make himself acceptable to God.

- Man can come to God only according to God's will and plan.

- Man must have faith in order to please God and be saved.

- The only way to please God is to trust that God is living His Life through you. Nothing less than perfection is acceptable to God. He is our Perfect Life, our only Life.

FOR CONSIDERATION

Allow God to remind you that He is your Life this week. Think through Jesus' desire to restore people's broken relationship with God. Ask Father to cause you to have a willingness to forgive both yourself, others or even God, as He lives through you as your Life.

CHAPTER 12
Salvation Accomplished!

Leviticus 17:11; 17:14;
Matthew 26:1-28:20; Mark 14:12 - 16:20;
Luke 19:28 - 24:53; John 18:1 - 20:31; Acts 17:28;
Hebrews 9:22 (NASB)

Jesus was now about to bring to fruition His whole purpose for coming into the world - to be mankind's Deliverer from sin, Satan and the world system that was under Satan's control. During the time of the Passover feast, Jesus rode into Jerusalem on a donkey just as Zechariah the prophet had predicted it. **Zechariah 9:9** People lined the streets to greet and welcome Him as their Deliverer. However, only a few days later, many of His own people would turn against Him.

On Thursday evening, Jesus gathered His disciples into an upper room to celebrate the Passover meal. During the meal, Jesus washed His disciples' feet to teach them how to live a life humble, surrendered and to lovingly serve one another. Bread and wine were elements of the Passover meal which reminded the Jewish people of God's deliverance of them when they were slaves in Egypt. It was also a foreshadowing of the Deliverer who would come and deliver them from slavery to sin. Jesus took the bread and broke it, explaining that it represented His body, which would be broken for all people.

This is the Body Side of the Cross - It is a symbol of receiving Jesus as our Life. In other words when we ask Jesus to be our Life, He does just that. He lives His Life through us. After all, He is the Life. *" Jesus said to him, 'I am the way, and the truth, and the life; no one comes to the Father but through Me.'"* **John 14:6** He is the essential part of this Life He has given us. Like the Passover, this bread represented the basic need of mankind - Jesus. He is the Bread of Life - that which is essential through the journey of the Christian Life. *"Jesus said to them, 'I am the bread of life; he who comes to Me will not hunger, and he who believes in Me will never thirst. This is the bread which came down out of heaven; not as the fathers ate and died; he who eats this bread will live forever.'"* **John 6:35, 58**

We need Him because only He can live the Christian Life. Jesus is living in us and through us. Jesus, represented by the Bread, is that sustenance that is essential in order to journey through our earthly existence. Again only He could live the Christian Life. That is why we need to rest in the finished work of Jesus. Jesus has accomplished everything that needed to be done. In faith we live as He lives through us, believing that He is working through us as we rest in Him. *"For in Him we live and move and have our being..."* **Acts 17:28(NIV)** He then took the cup of wine and drank it, explaining that it represented His blood, which would be shed for all people. This is called the Blood Side of the Cross - His blood was shed in order that we would be forgiven of all of our sins. Since "the life is in the blood," Jesus gave His Life for us. His Life paid for our sins. The innocent, for the guilty! *"For the life of a creature is in the blood..."* **Leviticus 17:11**

"...as for the life of all flesh, its blood is identified with its life...for the life of all flesh is its blood..." When Jesus shed His Blood, He gave His Whole Life! **Leviticus 17:14**

"And according to the Law, one may almost say, all things are cleansed with blood, and without shedding of blood there is no forgiveness." **Hebrews 9:22**

The penalty for sin is death - our death or His. Death is separation from God. We have to pay an eternity in hell for denying Jesus. Or, have faith in Jesus' the perfect, guilt-free and sinless sacrifice of God - the only way to heaven.

This represented the beginning of the New Covenant. Jesus then predicted that one of His 12 disciples would betray Him. He was speaking of Judas who had agreed to betray Jesus to the High Priest.

Jesus went out to the Garden of Gethsemane to pray. It was here that I think Jesus would find eternal perspective and the faith in God to endure what lay ahead. Knowing the agony that lay ahead of Him, Jesus was overwhelmed with grief. He asked His Father if His coming death could somehow be avoided. Yet He submitted to His Father saying, *"...not My will, but Yours be done."* **Luke 22:42** Later, Judas arrived with the Jewish leaders and soldiers who took Jesus away. The other disciples ran away in fear.

Jesus was brought before the Jewish leaders where He was falsely accused, mocked, spit upon and beaten. Although He had the power to overthrow His accusers, He did not even defend Himself. He willingly walked the path set before Him, the journey to the cross. He was taken to the Roman officer in charge, Pontius Pilate, who declared that He was innocent. However, the crowd shouted *"Crucify Him! Crucify Him!"* **Luke 23:21**

So Jesus was handed over to the Roman soldiers who scourged Him with a whip, beat Him and placed a crown of thorns on His head. Then, nailing Jesus' hands and feet to a cross, they crucified Him. As He hung on the cross, people mocked Him. Even in the midst of physical agony, Jesus' response was one of love. *"Father, forgive them, for they do not know what they are doing."* **Luke 23:34**

There were two thieves being crucified on either side of Jesus. One of them put his trust in Jesus as his Savior and Jesus promised him that he would enter paradise, or heaven, with Him. Just before He died, Jesus cried out *"...It is finished...!"* **John 19:30** This meant that He had fully satisfied God's wrath as punishment for people's sin. Jesus, the Lamb of God, died as a substitute for sinners.

At that moment, the veil in the temple, which covered the Holy of Holies, was torn from top to bottom. This signified that the barrier between God and man had been removed. The direction that it was split shows God's initiation of tearing down the barrier between God and mankind! Instead of being separated from God, He now lives in us! The Holy of Holies, that most sacred place, is in us to stay forever.

After Jesus' side was speared, He was buried in a tomb. A large stone was rolled in front of the tomb and several Roman soldiers guarded it closely. They were to make sure that no one would disturb the tomb or they would be put to death. Just as He had predicted, Jesus rose from the dead on the third day, Sunday. This act proved that He had conquered sin, death and Satan. It also showed that He was indeed the Son of God.

For forty days following His resurrection, Jesus lived on the earth appearing to His disciples and many others, teaching and instructing them. Then, having accomplished His purpose on earth as God's Deliverer, He ascended bodily into heaven. At this time, He instructed His disciples to wait in Jerusalem until the coming of the Holy Spirit.

"So when they [the disciples] *had come together, they were asking Him, saying, 'Lord, is it at this time You are restoring the kingdom to Israel?' He said to them, 'It is not for you to know times or epochs which the Father has fixed by His own authority; but you will receive power when the Holy Spirit has come upon you; and you shall be My witnesses both in Jerusalem, and in all Judea and Samaria, and even to the remotest part of the earth.' And after He had said these things, He was lifted up while they were looking on, and a cloud received Him out of their sight. And as they were gazing intently into the sky while He was going, behold, two men in white clothing stood beside them. They also said, 'Men of Galilee, why do you stand looking into the sky? This Jesus, who has been taken up from you into heaven, will come in just the same way as you have watched Him go into heaven'"* **Acts 1:6-11**

As we have seen throughout the Old Testament, God requires nothing less than death as the penalty for sin. However, God made a way for people to be forgiven of their sins. When people came to God in faith, recognizing their sin and trusting in His ability to forgive them, God forgave their sin. Often they sacrificed lambs and other animals as substitutes for themselves. This vividly pictured that God demanded death as the penalty for sin and that He was graciously accepting the death of another as payment for a person's sin debt.

Throughout His life, Jesus declared that He was God's Son and was equal to God. **John 10:30** He forgave people's sin, something only God could do. He also rose from the dead, something only God could do.

Part of that truth was that He would die as a substitute for sinners. The death of lambs never really paid for people's sins and as such, was never an adequate substitute for man. **Romans 3:21-26; Hebrews 10:1-4,11** Instead, the sacrifice of lambs was a picture of the one acceptable substitute that God Himself would provide - Jesus the Lamb of God.

When Jesus died on the cross He took the punishment for the sins of the whole world onto Himself. His death was the one and only sacrifice that could satisfy God's demands for death as the punishment for sin. **2Corinthians 5:21** says *"God made Him who had no sin to be sin for us, so that in Him we might become the righteousness of God."* When Jesus cried, *"...It is finished...!"* **John 19:30,** He proclaimed that He had completed His work as the substitute for sinners. Man's debt was fully paid and God was satisfied.

Jesus' resurrection dramatically demonstrated this truth. Satan could not keep Him in the grave and keep Him from reigning over the universe. He conquered death by the very act of rising from the dead. His resurrection demonstrated that He was truly the Son of God. This validated His claim that He was able to forgive sin, since only God can forgive sin. Because He conquered Satan, sin and death, He has given all believers this victory.

Many times, Jesus pronounced forgiveness of people's sins. In this chapter, He told the thief on the cross that he would go to heaven, thereby pronouncing that his sins had been forgiven. He told people that He was the way, the truth and the life and that whoever believes in Him would have eternal life **John 3:16; 5:24; 14:6.** By rising from the dead, Jesus proved that He was the Son of God and that all the things that He said must also be true. Thus, Jesus has the ability to forgive sins and give eternal life to all who trust in Him. He Himself is that Life!

Man's self-righteous, prideful heart can be seen in this chapter. The manner in which the people treated Jesus, the sinless Son of God, revealed their sinful condition. Just as we have seen in each chapter, man is unable to make himself acceptable to God. He cannot make himself clean. If he could, then God would not have sent a Deliverer, especially not His only Son, to rescue or save mankind. If man could save himself, Jesus would not have had to die on the cross.

Jesus' death and resurrection was the final culmination of God's glorious plan to save mankind and to bring people back to a relationship with Him. As we have seen in each chapter, God's plan is specific and man can only come to Him through His plan. If man tries to be saved in any other way God rejects him.

Many people in Jesus' day tried to be saved through religious effort. They relied upon their own righteousness and works to try to earn God's favor; but soon they discovered that God would reject their attempts to be righteous. Many people followed Jesus and claimed He was the Messiah, but they wanted Jesus to be their political/military King. They did not accept His spiritual teachings about eternal life. God rejected them because they did not accept and believe in His plan for salvation, but instead still held to their own. However, those who accepted Jesus' teachings and trusted in Him as their Deliverer were forgiven and accepted by God.

"Man is saved by faith alone" has been a consistent theme throughout the chapters. Faith means trusting when you have nothing else. Before people can trust Jesus as their Deliverer, they get to understand several things about God and themselves. They that they are sinners, that the punishment for their sin is death and their inability to make themselves acceptable to God.

God is holy, just and can rightly condemn them to eternal punishment in hell. God sent Jesus to be their substitute and Deliverer. Through trusting in Jesus and what He accomplished for them on the cross, they can be forgiven and given the gift of eternal life. **John 3:16; 5:24** Saving faith is simply trusting that what God has said about sin and its punishment is true for each of us and trusting in Jesus' death and resurrection as one's only means of salvation.

God had warned Adam and Eve in the Garden of Eden, that on the day they sinned against Him, they would surely die. **Genesis 2:17** The punishment for sin was death. Not only physical and spiritual death, but eternal death in hell. Throughout the Old Testament, God required nothing less than death as the penalty for sin. Because God is just, He must carry out this punishment on people because all are sinners. The only way people could escape this eternal death was if someone worthy enough died in their place. Then, God could still be just because their proper punishment would be carried out.

When Jesus died on the cross, He took the punishment for the sins of the whole world onto Himself. He was the substitute for all mankind. His death was the one and only sacrifice that could satisfy God's demands for death as the punishment for sin. Because He was God's

Son and lived a perfect life, He was worthy to bear the punishment for the sins of all people. That sin was so great that only God Himself could be a worthy substitute and only God could bear all of it!

Also, because Jesus was fully man, He could also qualify to be mankind's mediator or representative before Father. He could identify with mankind as to His humanness and identify with Father as to His perfect, holy, righteous standing as God. This made it possible for Him to approach Father on behalf of sinful people. If God had not sent Jesus to be man's Savior and if Jesus had not willingly gone to the cross, all people would still be under the condemnation of eternal punishment. No one could be saved and all would enter hell after physical death.

The severities of Jesus physical sufferings are directly related to the degree of man's sinfulness. Jesus certainly could have died a quick, painless death. But instead, He died a cruel, painful, agonizing, shameful death. Jesus became sin for us in the sense that God's entire wrath against sin and sinners was unleashed upon Jesus on the cross. **2Corinthians 5:21**

God treated Jesus how He should have treated us. This shows the utter sinfulness of people, since Jesus had to suffer so much in order to satisfy God's wrath. He didn't just pay for one person's sins; He paid for the sins of everyone who ever lived and whoever will live! Regarding man's sinfulness, it has been said that we are no better than what Jesus had to become for us on the cross. Since we are all so prone to think of ourselves self-righteously, the above statements are a healthy reminder of the depths of our sin. The good news is that God's grace is greater than all of our sin and that Jesus' death was sufficient to satisfy God's demands for justice.

"The Law came in so that the transgression would increase; but where sin increased, grace abounded all the more, so that, as sin reigned in death, even so grace would reign through righteousness to eternal life through Jesus Christ our Lord." **Romans 5:20-21**

Jesus' resurrection is important because forgiveness of sins and God's whole plan of redemption hinges upon it. Jesus' resurrection proves that He was the Son of God because only God could raise Himself from the dead. It also shows that Jesus' words are trustworthy because He predicted that He would rise from the dead. If Jesus had not risen from the dead, then He would be no different than any other religious leader - still dead in the grave. His claims to be the Son of God would have to be dismissed.

He would not have power over Satan, sin and death if He Himself did not conquer death. He would not be a risen Savior who reigns over the earth, but a dead, misguided, false prophet. Christians would still not have forgiveness of sins. As Paul said, *"and if Christ has not been raised, your faith is worthless; you are still in your sins."* **1Corimthians 15:17** Jesus also said that He would come again to judge the world. Since He is risen and living and His words are trustworthy, He will indeed come again.

The resurrection has tremendous significance for Christian living. Jesus had explained to His disciples that it would actually be better for them if He went away. **John 16:7** This shows that Jesus could then come to live inside of them through His Holy Spirit. **John 14:16-20;**

15:1-5 If Jesus had not risen from the dead, He would not be able to live inside of His children. The effect of having God actually living inside of all believers will be discussed further in Chapters 13 & 14.

SUMMARY

- God is holy, righteous and demands death as the penalty for sin.

- Jesus is God's Son and is equal to God.

- Jesus, the Lamb of God, died as a substitute for sinners.

- Jesus has power over Satan, sin and death.

- Jesus forgives sins and gives people eternal life.

- Unsaved man is a sinner and cannot make himself acceptable to God.

- Man can come to God only according to God's will and plan.

- Man must have faith in order to please God and be saved.

- The only way to please God is to trust that God is living His Life through you. Nothing less than perfection is acceptable to God. He is our Perfect Life, our only Life.

FOR CONSIDERATION

Allow God to remind you that He is your Life this week. Reflect upon Jesus' willingness to be publicly abused, humiliated and crucified because of His personal love for you.

CHAPTER 13
The Birth & Growth of the Church

Genesis 12:3; John 1:29-35; 16:5-15;
Acts 1:1- 4:37; 7:54 - 8:3; 9:1-31; 10:34-48; 17:16-34;
Acts 28:17-31

After Jesus was crucified and rose from the dead, He spent 40 days instructing and ministering to the eleven apostles and many other believers. Knowing that His followers could do nothing apart from God's supernatural working, He told them to wait in Jerusalem for the promised Holy Spirit, saying; *"...you will receive power when the Holy Spirit comes on you and you will be My witnesses in Jerusalem and in all Judea and Samaria and to the ends of the earth."* **Acts 1:8**

In the Old Testament God had focused primarily on His people, the Israelites. Now the message of salvation that came through the Jewish people was to be brought to all nations, just as God had promised in **Genesis 12:3.** Father's intent was to always reach all people. In the Old Testament, the Israelites were to be an example of a people who followed God. Through the nation of Israel, those who did not know God heard the stories of all that Father did throughout the different lands. Even then, if they had repented and asked to be among those who believe in Him, Father would have granted it.

Scripture is full, of accounts where those who were not Israeli would be saved as well: the prostitute Rahab in **Joshua 2:8-15** The King of Babylon King Nebuchadnezzar also was saved and worshiped Father **Daniel chapter 4.** In the book of **Ruth**, Ruth was a Moabite woman, she too was adopted into the family of God, **Ruth chapter 4**

In the New Testament, Father intended to reach the world through the Israelites. As a people, they rejected Jesus. We read in **Romans 11:11-12** *"I say then, they did not stumble so as to fall, did they? May it never be! But by their transgression salvation has come to the Gentiles, to make them jealous. Now if their transgression is riches for the world and their failure is riches for the Gentiles, how much more will their fulfillment be! After Jesus spoke, ...He was lifted up while they were looking on, and a cloud received Him out of their sight."* **Acts 1:9**, He ascended into heaven to sit at the right hand of God the Father.

JERUSALEM

The spread of the Gospel throughout Jerusalem occurred several days later, on the Day of Pentecost. The apostles were all gathered in one place when the Holy Spirit came upon them. They were filled with the Holy Spirit and began to speak in other tongues or languages. The crowd was amazed because each foreigner heard the apostles speak in their own language. Peter addressed the crowd, preaching about the crucifixion and resurrection of Jesus.

He instructed the people to repent so that they could receive forgiveness of sins and the gift of the Holy Spirit. People's hearts were moved with sorrow over their sin. About 3000 believed in Jesus that day and were saved. In the days that followed the believer's fellowshipped together daily and generously shared their belongings with one another. The message of God's grace to sinners had melted many hearts and God performed signs and wonders through the apostles. The miraculous work of the Holy Spirit was so evident in the believers' lives *"...And the Lord was adding to their number day by day those who were being saved."*

Acts 2:47

JUDEA & SAMARIA

God used persecution to force the believers to scatter and spread the Gospel to surrounding areas. Most of the Jewish people, particularly the religious leaders, refused to open their hearts and instead persecuted the apostles. As people fled for their lives Father used them to share *"the Life of* Jesus. The apostles continued to preach in the temples saying; *"²⁰...we cannot help speaking about what we have seen and heard"* **Acts 4:20**. The Jews were so furious that they stoned one of the believers, Stephen. The Jewish leader Saul witnessed and gave approval to this murder. On that day, the persecution in Jerusalem grew so intense that all believers except the apostles were scattered throughout Judea and Samaria. **Acts 8:1**

THE ENDS OF THE EARTH

Sometime later, Saul was miraculously converted while on the road to Damascus. A fierce and determined persecutor of Christians, Saul was transformed by an encounter with Jesus Himself. God chose Saul - later called Paul - to be His instrument to bring the Gospel to the Gentiles. **Acts 9:15** Paul and others traveled great distances and visited many cities to bring the good news of Jesus to other Jewish people and Gentiles. God used His servants to start and establish many new churches, some in areas as far as Rome. The Holy Spirit was truly at work!

God controls the events in the book of Acts. He sovereignly sent the Holy Spirit to the apostles during a time when many foreigners were in Jerusalem for the

Feast of Pentecost. He performs many signs and wonders through the apostles. He delivered some of them from prison. Jesus miraculously confronted Saul on the road to Damascus. Through the entire book of Acts, one can see how God led the early church through His Holy Spirit.

Through His spokesmen, God offered the gift of forgiveness and eternal life to any who believed in Jesus. Even those who had supported Jesus' death were given an opportunity for forgiveness (Saul for instance). God's grace is especially evident in His calling of Saul who later called himself the worst of all sinners. **1Timothy 1:15**

After spending 40 days with His disciples, Jesus ascended bodily into heaven, **Acts 1:1-9**, to be at the right hand of His Father. **Acts 7:56** Jesus was seated at the right hand of God the Father showing that He was equal to the Father. He too was and is God the Son! God did not leave Jesus' followers alone to fend for themselves. He did not simply give them instructions and wish them the best of luck.

Jesus had told the apostles that apart from Him, they could do nothing in **John 15:5.** So He instructed them to wait in Jerusalem for the promised Holy Spirit. This period of waiting was probably another reinforcer to the apostles that they were helpless to do anything for God apart from Him miraculously working in and through them.

The Holy Spirit was sent to indwell and empower every believer. **Romans 8:9; 1Corinthians 3:16** Throughout the book of Acts, there are constant references to the Spirit's leading of the early church. The Holy Spirit is called the Counselor. He reveals the Truth (Jesus) to us. All that we receive, we receive through revelation by the Holy Spirit. Jesus lives His Life through us.

The apostles did not preach that man could save himself by obeying the Law or by good works, but that mankind were sinners under God's condemnation. **Acts 2:38; 3:19; 7:51-53** The apostles preached that only through Jesus could sinful man be saved. **Acts 4:10-12** The apostles' message was to repent and believe or simply to believe. **Acts 2:38; 16:31.** To repent literally means to change one's mind. The people particularly the Jewish people, needed to change their minds about Jesus. They needed to believe that He truly was the Deliverer or Messiah, and that He came to die for their sins.

They needed to believe that they could not come to God through obeying the Law, but only through faith in Jesus. If someone says they believe in Jesus but is still not convicted of their sin or is trusting in their good works for salvation, they really have not changed their former way of thinking. They may have not repented or at least are still struggling with their flesh patterns.

Some Christians, most notably the Church of Christ denomination, have interpreted verses like **Acts 2:38** and **Mark 16:16** to mean that baptism is necessary for salvation. An initial glance at these verses would seem to support this view. However, when formulating any biblical doctrine, all of Scripture must be considered. Every story in this material has taught that faith is the only requirement for salvation. It is clear from Scripture that man can do absolutely nothing to add to the finished work of Jesus.

In scripture, Jesus is seen in a sitting position at the right hand of the Father. He is seated because there is nothing left to do - He did all that was necessary. If there is still any doubt, Jesus puts it to rest by declaring, *"...it is finished..."* **John 19:30** In fact, the thief in **Luke 23: 26-43** was told by Jesus *"...I assure you, today you will be with Me in paradise."* The thief was not baptized. Even baptism is not a requirement to "get into heaven." Yes we are to be baptized in obedience to Jesus. Baptism is an outward symbolic action identifying with Jesus' death. The believer is saying that he/she has been crucified with Christ, born again, and raised with Christ. It truly is finished.

There are over 150 verses in Scripture which clearly state that salvation is through faith alone. **John 3:16; Ephesians 2:8-9; etc** As already mentioned, baptism is only an external action, which symbolizes the internal change that has already taken place in a believer. Believers should be baptized because Jesus commanded it and it is a powerful testimony to both believers and unbelievers. It was mostly done in public as a testimony of the believer agreeing that He has died in Christ. *"I have been crucified with Christ; and it is no longer I who live, but Christ lives in me; and the life which I now live in the flesh I live by faith in the Son of God, who loved me and gave Himself up for me."* **Galatians 2:20**

The chapters in the Old Testament clearly showed that all people have a sin nature. Their hearts are evil and selfish. They are also spiritually dead. They are unable in themselves to produce good works and righteousness. If God did nothing more than simply forgive their sins, people would still be spiritually dead with an evil heart. They would be unable in themselves to live righteously. God knew that all people needed radical heart surgery and He graciously promised to give people a new heart and a new spirit in **Ezekiel 36:25-28.**

Jesus also taught that people were unable by themselves to produce any good fruit in **John 15:1-17**. In the Old Testament, the Jewish people were often referred to as a fruitless vine as in **Jeremiah 2:21** and **Haggai 2:19**. In **John 15:5**, Jesus introduced a revolutionary concept. He declared; *"Yes, I am the vine; you are the branches. Those who remain in Me, and I in them, will produce much fruit. For apart from Me, you can do nothing.'"* Jesus, through the Holy Spirit, lives in each believer **Galatians 2:20.** One of God's gifts to the believer is the indwelling Holy Spirit through whom good fruit is produced as the believer yields and trusts in Jesus Who indwells him. **Galatians 2:20; 5:22-23**

The effect of the Holy Spirit on the believers was powerful. This same power is still in effect today. They were transformed from being uncertain and afraid to being bold and outspoken. Their own determination and resolve had obviously failed them previously as in Peter's denial of Christ. This new boldness was a supernatural work of God. They were also drawn together in love as the Spirit transformed the hearts of many new believers.

This new community of diverse people loving one another was a powerful testimony to unbelievers. It was also one of the reasons for the rapid growth of the church in **Acts 2:42-47**. The Holy Spirit also personally guided and led Paul and others on their missionary journeys. **Acts 11:12; 13:4; 20:22**. Jesus had told His disciples that He would build His church, **Matthew 16:18**, and He did this through His Holy Spirit living in each believer and working on the hearts of unbelievers. As Paul later wrote, God used people to spread the

Gospel, but it was God Who caused the growth of the church. **1Corinthians 3:6**

In response to Peter's sermon on the Day of Pentecost, the people were *"Peter's words pierced their hearts"* **Acts 2:37**. They realized that they were sinners and stood guilty before God. They deserved punishment for their sin. This message about Jesus was not another religious message about trying to please God. It was Great News! Forgiveness of sins and eternal life were freely offered to all. The good news became the whole focus of the new believers. *"All the believers devoted themselves to the apostles' teaching, and to fellowship, and to sharing in meals (including the Lord's Supper), and to prayer."* **Acts 2:42**

They were also focused on telling others this good news. "And each day the Lord added to their fellowship those who were being saved." **Acts 2:47** Their supernaturally encouraged response to God's grace being showered upon them was to show love and grace toward one another. Their eyes were off of themselves and on the Lord. They were truly grateful to God for His love, mercy and grace.

In this day and age, many preachers of the gospel are televised. With this popularity, if the preacher does not point people to Jesus and off of himself/herself, people begin to focus on the speaker rather than the Spoken About - Jesus. This can lead to personality cults - where the preacher is worshipped instead of the True Life - Jesus. This is what John the Baptist did when he pointed people to Jesus. *"The next day John saw Jesus coming toward him and said, 'Look! The Lamb of God Who takes away the sin of the world! He is the One I was talking about when I said, 'A Man is coming after me*

Who is far greater than I am, for He existed long before me.' I did not recognize Him as the Messiah, but I have been baptizing with water so that He might be revealed to Israel. Then John testified, 'I saw the Holy Spirit descending like a dove from heaven and resting upon Him. I didn't know He was the One, but when God sent me to baptize with water, He told me, 'The One on Whom you see the Spirit descend and rest is the One Who will baptize with the Holy Spirit.' I saw this happen to Jesus, so I testify that He is the Chosen One of God.'"
John 1:29-35

Although God had promised in **Genesis 12:3** that all nations would be blessed through the Jewish people, God mainly interacted with Jewish people in the Old Testament. Jesus also concerned Himself primarily with the Jewish people. **Matthew 15:24**. Although there are instances in the Old Testament in which Gentiles came to believe in God, the Jewish people had a special relationship with God. They were His chosen people.

God had given the Jewish people the Law and God lived in their temple. Thus, if someone wanted to know their God, they had to adopt the Jewish faith with all its rituals and customs. In the Jewish mindset, they were God's favorites. Much like a child might believe a parent favors him over another sibling. They looked down on the Gentiles, often treating them as inferiors. In fact, many of them considered Gentiles to be their enemies and God's enemies.

To suggest that Gentiles now had equal access to God was radical. That is why God had to use a dramatic vision and an incident at Cornelius' house in **Acts 10**, to convince the Jewish believers that "... [34] God shows no favoritism." **Acts 10:34** God was granting the Gentiles an equal opportunity to believe in Jesus and receive eternal life. Later, in **Acts 15**, God led a church council in Jerusalem to decide that Gentile believers were not required to adopt any Jewish custom because salvation came by faith alone in Jesus Christ, not through obeying the Law.

The Life of Jesus would flow through all who accepted His sacrifice of His death, as full payment for their sins. Jesus would be the sustenance for their journey to the Father's Heart. This is called "the body side of the cross." It is a picture of communion much like that of the Passover.

"So Jesus said again, 'I tell you the truth, unless you eat the flesh of the Son of Man and drink His blood, you cannot have eternal life within you. But anyone who eats My flesh and drinks My blood has eternal life, and I will raise that person at the last day. For My flesh is true food, and My blood is true drink. Anyone who eats My flesh and drinks My blood remains in Me, and I in him. I live because of the living Father Who sent Me; in the same way, anyone who feeds on Me will live because of Me. I Am the true bread that came down from heaven. Anyone who eats this bread will not die as your ancestors did (even though they ate the manna) but will live forever.' He said these things while He was teaching in the synagogue in Capernaum." **John 6:53-59**

SUMMARY

- God is sovereign.

- God is loving, merciful and gracious.

- God sent the Holy Spirit to indwell, guide and empower believers.

- Unsaved man is a sinner and cannot make himself acceptable to God.

- Man can come to God only according to God's will and plan.

- Mankind must have faith in order to please God and be saved.

FOR CONSIDERATION

Allow God to cause you to meditate on the fact that He has given you His Holy Spirit to live inside of you. He empowers you to live by God's grace and is your Counselor. **John 16:7**

CHAPTER 14
The Establishment & Maturing of the Church

Matthew 7:21-23; 26:24; John 1:14-18; 5:24; 10:9-10;
John 10:27-28;17:12; 19:30; Acts 15:41; 18:23; 22:14;
Romans 1-5; 6:1-14; 7:21-25; 8:1-11; 2Peter 1:3-4;
1Corinthians 3:10-15; Galatians2:15-21;
2Corinthians 1:21-22; 3:4-11; 4:5; 5:17-21;
Galatians 2:20; 3:1-5; 5:16-25; 3:6-25;5:1-4; 1:6-12;
Ephesians 6:10-18; 1:3-23; 2:1-22; 1John 1:9; 5:13
Philippians 1:6; 2:12-13; 3:10-14;
Colossians 1:25-29; 2:1-15; 3:1-4; 4:16;
2Thessalonians 2:15; 1Timothy 3:1-15; Titus 1:5-9;
Hebrews 8:6-13; 9:15; James 4:7; 1Peter 1:3-5;

In the previous chapter, the Holy Spirit was poured out on the Day of Pentecost and the early church was born. The apostles and others travelled great distances to spread the Gospel and many churches were established. These new believers and new churches needed to have a strong foundation in their Christian faith **1Corinthians 3:10-15**. So Paul and others visited many cities with the purpose of *"...strengthening the churches."* **Acts 15:41**

The new Christians also had a tremendous need for writings, which could instruct them in the faith. At this time their "Bible" consisted of only the Old Testament because the New Testament had not yet been written. The teachings of Jesus had been passed on orally because neither Jesus nor His disciples recorded His teachings nor the events of His life while Jesus was alive. After Jesus died, the Holy Spirit inspired the writers of the Gospels to compose several accounts of His life. The Holy Spirit also inspired Paul and others to compose letters of instruction, correction and encouragement to the early believers. These letters were often written when a personal visit to a church was not possible.

The 21 books of the Bible from **Romans** to **Jude** are all letters or epistles, written by individuals to other individuals or churches. All of the letters were copied and circulated to other churches and eventually became the major portion of the New Testament. The books are named after the person or church to whom they were written, such as **1&2Timothy and Romans**. Or, they are named for their author, such as **1&2Peter or James**. The subjects vary from book to book.

But the theme is constant throughout - Jesus is our Deliverer. The story has been and is about Him. It is History or if you will, His-story. For example, **Romans** explains the foundations of the Gospel. **Galatians** was written to defend the Gospel of grace and to combat legalism. **1Corinthians** was written to correct problems in the church at Corinth. **1Peter** was written to encourage suffering Christians. All of the writings have Jesus as the answer to all of mankind's problems.

Paul wrote thirteen of the 21 letters. Paul was specially chosen not only to preach the Gospel to the Gentiles, but to be the one through whom God would reveal spiritual mysteries that had been *"...the mystery which has been hidden from the past ages and generations..."* **Colossians 1:26** Since the fall of Adam and Eve, God had progressively revealed Himself to mankind. The ultimate revelation of Himself came through His Son Jesus, *"...but God's unfailing love and faithfulness came through Jesus Christ..."* **John 1:14-18(NLT)**

God then chose Paul, among others, to explain how Jesus' death and resurrection could not only save people but could "exchange" their daily lives for His. Instead of walking around dead in their sins, they could truly experience the abundant life that Jesus talks about. **John 10:9-10** Jesus exchanges our old, dead life for His very Life. He lives through us.

Jesus spoke to Paul directly, **Acts 22:14**, and explained to him many important truths. Paul's goal was to proclaim Christ, **2Corinthians 4:5**, to believers and unbelievers so that all people would be reconciled to God through Jesus. *"Therefore if anyone is in Christ, he is a new creature; the old things passed away; behold, new things have come. Now all these things are from God, who reconciled us to Himself through Christ and gave us the ministry of reconciliation, namely, that God was in Christ reconciling the world to Himself, not counting their trespasses against them, and He has committed to us the word of reconciliation. Therefore, we are ambassadors for Christ, as though God were making an appeal through us; we beg you on behalf of Christ, be reconciled to God."* **2Corinthians 5:17-20**

God's strength through Paul was sufficient for the task. **2Corinthians 3:4-5; Colossians 1:27-29.** Many believers in his day and ours have been strengthened and encouraged through his and the other apostles' letters.

JUSTIFICATION BY FAITH
Romans 1-5

In the book of **Romans,** "justification by faith" is an important theme. One way in which the American Heritage Dictionary defines "justify" is; "to declare free of blame, absolve." Another simple definition is "to declare righteous". To justify does not mean to make righteous or to pretend someone is righteous. It means to give someone a righteous standing, regardless of their true guilt. God not only forgives people of their sin, He also declares them totally righteous. The perfect, righteous life that Jesus lived is credited or imputed to the sinner's account when they trust in Jesus as their Savior. This righteousness is from God and is received by faith;

Romans 1:17; 3:21 It is a gift from God given by His Grace. It has nothing to do with one's personal conduct. This righteous standing is a foundational element of each believer's "position in Christ" or "who we are in Christ". So we are made righteous as new creations and we are declared righteous in Christ.
2Corinthians 5:17

We are justified. We are treated as if we never sinned. It is based on who we are in Him. At the core of our being, in our spirit, we are a finished product of God's creation. We are holy, blameless, righteous, and pure; everything Father intended us to be. Our spirit is one with God's Spirit - inseparable!

All believers receive this righteousness at salvation. They are forever seen righteous in God's eyes. It is as if Jesus won a gold medal and places it around the neck of each believer. It is as if He received a score of 100 in His life on earth and the 100 is placed in each believer's account. Whether you see yourself receiving a 20 or a 90 in this life, it does not matter. He gives a score of 100 to all who trust in Jesus as their Life.

Sadly, many Christians go through life thinking that God is still judging them on a 0-100 scale. They might believe that they are saved, but they still live under the burden of trying to be "good enough" to please God. Life is always a struggle and full of defeat for these Christians. They are not living in light of their daily righteous standing before God. Instead, they are offering to God their own performance and attempts to live righteously. God has provided for them a totally righteous standing in Christ, yet they are still trying to offer Him their own righteousness. This attitude and action shows a failure to recognize God's demands for total righteousness, man's inability to produce righteousness and God's gracious act of justification.

The life of a perfect Christian is the only acceptable life to God. That perfect Christian is the one whom it was named after, Christ. As we rest in the fact, by faith that Jesus is living His life through us, we are living the Christian Life. Anything of eternal value must come from Him and Him alone. Unsaved man is a sinner and cannot make himself acceptable to God. God will reject any of man's attempts to do so. The only way God can accept people is if they are declared totally righteous. Anything less than perfect righteousness is unacceptable to the Holy and Perfect God.

When people offer their own righteousness to God, in effect they are saying that they do not need Christ's righteousness in order to have relationship with God. Living in light of one's righteous standing before God is critical for growing in the Christian life. It is a matter of surrendering all control of every aspect of life to Father. Jesus can only accomplish it.

JUSTIFICATION BECAUSE OF PROPITIATION
Romans 3:25-26

Since God is holy, righteous and demands death as the penalty for sin, how can He declare sinners righteous and remain just? The answer is given in **Romans 3:21-26**. Although God had accepted sinners through faith in the Old Testament, the sacrificing of animals never really paid for people's sins and God would not be just if He allowed their sins to remain unpunished. It was necessary for Jesus to come and to take all of mankind's punishment on Himself in order for God to be able to forgive sinners and still remain just.

God graciously gave of Himself when He presented Jesus as the solution to man's problem. Jesus was a propitiation sacrifice or atonement. To propitiate means to appease or satisfy. As mentioned in Chapter four, atonement is at-one-ment. Being at one with Father through faith in His Ultimate Sacrifice - Jesus. *"I do not ask on behalf of these alone, but for those also who believe in Me through their word; that they may all be one; even as You, Father, are in Me and I in You, that they also may be in Us, so that the world may believe that You sent Me."* **John 17:20-21**

God's wrath on sinners, which had been "in check" until the time of Jesus, was fully unleashed on Jesus during His painful crucifixion. God did not hold back but vented His entire wrath on Jesus who was our substitute, for the past; the present; and the future. After Jesus said *"...It is finished..."*, God was propitiated or satisfied. **John 19:30**

Now, through Christ's work on the cross, believers have peace with God and can live each day without fear of punishment from God. **Romans 5:1** Knowing this can release one from fear of failure and free oneself to serve God with joy. If you (more accurately, the flesh) sin, all you need to do is admit it to our loving, gracious Father and thank Him that it has already been forgiven in Jesus. As it says in **1John 1:9** *"If we confess our sins, He is faithful and righteous to forgive us our sins and to cleanse us from all unrighteousness."*

ETERNAL SECURITY
2 Corinthians 1:21-22; 1Peter 1:3-5;
John 5:24; 10:27-28; 1John 5:13

God's gift of eternal life can never be lost, taken away or given back to God. The phrase "once saved, always saved" describes this wonderful biblical truth. This is another foundational truth for spiritual growth. Believers who lack assurance of their salvation have tremendous difficulty growing spiritually. Without the security of knowing that God has already accepted them in Christ, they often struggle to maintain a favorable standing with God. They cannot fully appreciate God's love and grace because they are unsure whether God will ultimately accept or reject them.

The Bible also teaches that there are some people who appear to be saved but who are in reality unsaved. They may appear to be Christians for a while but later reject God and His truth. Some of these people could be "backslidden" or "carnal" Christians and some could be unsaved. Only God knows each person's heart. An example is Judas, one of the 12 apostles, who betrayed Jesus. Certainly he must have appeared to be a believer because no one accused him when Jesus declared that He was about to be betrayed.

In fact, he was the treasurer, an office of trust and respect. Yet Jesus said that it would have been better if Judas had never been born. **Matthew 26:24** Jesus said that he was doomed to destruction in **John 17:12**. Judas did not lose his salvation. It appears he was never saved. Those who profess Jesus in words, but who are really not saved are described as having made a "false profession" of faith. Jesus described these people in **Matthew 7:21-23**. *"Not everyone who says to Me, 'Lord, Lord,' will enter the kingdom of heaven, but he*

*who does the will of My Father who is in heaven will
enter. Many will say to Me on that day, 'Lord, Lord, did
we not prophesy in Your Name, and in Your Name cast
out demons, and in Your Name perform many miracles?'
And then I will declare to them, 'I never knew you;
DEPART FROM ME, YOU WHO PRACTICE LAWLESSNESS.'"*

One's assurance of salvation should never be based on
one's feelings or emotions but on one's belief in the
truths of the Gospel. Jesus is that truth. All believers
experience times of spiritual dryness, which causes
many to unnecessarily question their salvation. If you
ever question your salvation, review the truths learned in
God's Word and reaffirm your trust in Jesus' death and
resurrection as your only hope of salvation. Review the
verses listed for eternal security and trust in God's
Word, not your feelings.

So we are made righteous as new creations and we are
declared righteous in Christ. **2Corinthians 5:17** We are
justified - We are treated as if we never sinned. It is
based on who we are in Him. At the core of our being,
in our spirit, we are a finished product of God's creation.
We are holy, blameless, righteous, and pure; everything
Father intended us to be. Our spirit is one with God's
Spirit - inseparable!

When realizing that we have given into the flesh, we do
not need to ask for forgiveness. We have been forgiven
of every past, present and future sin we will ever
commit. We simply need to confess or agree with God
that it was sin and thank Him for His forgiveness. It is a
declaration of what has already happened.

Jesus made this possible by His death on the cross. He
paid the price of our disobedience. He became sin for
us, so that we would become the righteousness of God.

His resurrection shows that He was victorious over sin, Satan and the world system. His victory became ours. God's gift of eternal life can never be lost, taken away or given back to God.

SUMMARY

- God has reconciled people back to Himself.

- God's wrath has been satisfied through the death of Jesus.

- God can forgive sinners of all their sins and declare them righteous.

- God gives believers spiritual life through the indwelling Holy Spirit.

- God offers salvation as a free gift, which can never be lost or stolen.

- Man receives salvation through faith alone and not by works.

- Believers grow in their Christian life by grace through faith.

FOR CONSIDERATION

Allow God to remind you that He is your only Life this week. Thank Him for the fact that He has given you emotions. Thank Him also that you do not have to depend on your emotions to tell you whether you are saved or not. Thank Him that He is the Truth and that what He says about you is true and not based on how you feel.

CHAPTER 15
Who You Are In Christ
Law vs Grace

Deuteronomy 27:26; 28; Jeremiah 3; Matthew 9:16-17;
John 1:16-17;Romans 7:4-25; 12:1;
2Corinthians 1:21-22; 3:7-9; 5:17-21;
Galatians 1:6-12; 2:15-21; 3:6-27; 5:1-4;
Ephesians 1:3-23; 2:1-22; 6:10-18; Colossians 2:20-23;
1Timothy 3:1-15; Titus 1:5-9; 2:11; 1John 4:19
Hebrews 8:6-13; 9:15; 10:3; James 4:7; 2Peter 3:18;

Jeremiah had prophesied about the coming New
Covenant in **Jeremiah 31**. Jesus described it in terms of
new wine and new wineskins in **Matthew 9:16-17**. God
used Paul and the author of Hebrews to fully explain the
New Covenant or Covenant of Grace, which began when
Christ died, rose again and sent the Holy Spirit.

God introduced the Law or Old Covenant during the
time of Moses for a specific purpose. The two fold
purpose of the Law was to show God's holiness and
man's sinfulness. **Romans 7:4-25** The reason it was
added was because of transgressions, **Galatians 3:19**
because people were sinners in need of grace and
forgiveness. God introduced the Law so that people
would be more likely to recognize their sin and turn to
God for His mercy. Those in the Old Testament who
recognized their sin and trusted in God's mercy to
forgive them were declared righteous and accepted by
God. **Galatians 3:6-8**

However, the Law did not justify or declare anyone
righteous. Instead, it magnified people's sin and
condemned them because *"Cursed is he who does not
confirm the words of this law by doing them.' And all the*

people shall say, 'Amen.'" **Deuteronomy 27:26; Galatians 3:10** That is why Paul describes the Law as the *"...ministry that brought death... brought condemnation..."* **2Corinthians 3:7-9**

Although God provided mercy and grace through the Old Testament sacrificial system, those sacrifices were a constant reminder of sin, **Hebrews 10:3.** The sacrifices were a representation of how the coming Deliverer was to deal with our sin. The people lived under the constant reminder that they did not measure up to God's standard and that God's curse could come upon them at any time.

It was actually very loving for God to have introduced the Law because through the Law comes the knowledge of sin and therefore an awareness of the need for forgiveness **Romans 7:7**. The Law was added *"...* [19] until the Seed would come to whom the promise had been made."* **Galatians 3:19** This seed is Jesus. **Genesis 3:14-15** Although people in the Old Testament were always saved by grace through faith, once Christ came and died, it could be clearly seen that salvation was a gift from God that could only be received through faith. The Law was put into effect from Moses to Christ and it accomplished its purpose. Paul declared; *"...But now that faith has come, we are no longer under a tutor..."* **Galatians 3:22-27**

Since the death and resurrection of Christ, all believers have been under the New Covenant. It is foremost a covenant of grace. While in the Old Covenant blessings were conditional upon one's obedience to the Law. **Deuteronomy 28** In the New Covenant, the believer receives every spiritual blessing through faith in Christ at the time of salvation **John 1:16-17; Ephesians 1:3**. God has put His laws in people's minds and on their hearts as He promised in **Jeremiah 31:31-34** and **Hebrews 8:8-12.**

Our Position in Christ

In this chapter, we will give a partial listing of the blessings that all Christians have received at salvation. These blessings are not a result of any works or performance by man. They are all received by faith at the time of salvation. The phrase "position in Christ" refers to each believer's standing before God. God sees all believers as "in Christ" because they are clothed with the righteousness of Christ. **Galatians 3:27**

He sees them as forgiven, declared righteous, and made righteous as new creations no matter what their actual spiritual "condition" on earth. Although while we live on earth our "condition" fluctuates, God sees us in light of our "position" because He sees us "in Christ". As already mentioned, Father treats us according to our identity not our actions. Though in the earthly realm we are in process, God sees us in our final state of being. God is not stuck or limited by time. He is eternal and encompasses all eternity. Past, present and future are terms that may be applied to us. But with God, everything is now! He sees past, present and future as now. He can intervene in time but He is not contained by or limited by it.

Living in light of this truth can drastically change one's relationship with God because the believer can rest assured that his standing before Father never changes. His standing is based on his position in Christ, which is the same for all believers. Your position is now eternally appraised. Your standing is not based on your performance or ability to live the Christian life.

Understanding these truths is what motivates believers to live righteously out of gratitude and security. We don't need to emphasize rules, laws or principles to obey. **Colossians 2:20-23; Titus 2:11** Paul said that the love of Christ compelled him. **2Corinthians 5:14** In **1John 4:19**, John wrote; *"we love because He first loved us."*

Genuine growth as a Christian comes in response to understanding and growing in God's love and grace, **2Peter 3:18; Romans 12:1.** A way to gain a fuller appreciation of God's love and grace is to first grow in one's understanding of other aspects of God's nature and character such as His holiness, sovereignty and justice.

The phrase "position in Christ" refers to each believer's standing before God. God sees all believers as "in Christ" because they are clothed with the righteousness of Christ. **Galatians 3:27** God says that you are deeply loved; completely forgiven; fully pleasing; totally accepted and absolutely complete in Christ. Therefore, *Father treats us according to our new identity not our actions.*

TRUE BELIEVERS IN JESUS...

have been blessed with every spiritual blessing in Christ. **Ephesians 1:3**

have been given everything they need for life & godliness. **2Peter 1:3**

have been justified or declared righteous. **Romans 5:1**

have peace with God. **Romans 5:2**

have died with Christ & been resurrected to new Life. **Romans 6:1-6** are free forever from condemnation.   **Romans 8:1**

have been forgiven of all their sin. **Colossians 1:14, 2:13-14**

have been given the gift of eternal life. **John 3:16; 5:24; 1John 5:13**

have Christ living in them through the Holy Spirit. **1Corinthians 3:16; Galatians 2:20; Colossians 3:4**

are recipients of God's lavish grace.   **Ephesians 1:7-8**

are seated with Christ in the heavenly realms. **Ephesians 1:6**

are chosen by God & dearly loved. **Colossians 3:12; 1Thessalonians 1:4**

may approach God with boldness, freedom & confidence. **Ephesians 3:12; Hebrews 4:16**

have been given an inheritance in heaven that can never perish, spoil or fade. **1Peter 1:3-4**

have a place for them in heaven prepared by Jesus. **John 14:2**

have been rescued from the domain of darkness - or Satan's rule - and transferred to the kingdom of Christ. **Colossians 1:13**

have spiritual armor to stand against the devil's schemes. **Ephesians 6:10-18**

have Christ's power in them to defeat Satan.   **1John 4:4**

Identity of all Believers

TRUE BELIEVERS IN JESUS...

are children of God. God is their Daddy. **John 1:12; Romans 8:14-16**

are Christ's friend and brother. **John 15:15; Hebrews 2:11**

are joint-heirs with Christ, sharing His inheritance with Him. **Romans 8:17**

are saints. **Ephesians 1:1**

are vessels containing God's Spirit. **1Corinthians 3:16; 2Corinthians 4:7**

are branches or channels, connected to the true vine, Jesus, Who is the source of life. **John 15:1-5**

are a chosen people, a royal priesthood, a holy nation, a people belonging to God. **1Peter 2:9-10**

are new creations. **2Corinthians 5:17**

are citizens of heaven and seated in heaven right now. **Philippians 3:20; Ephesians 2:6**

are Christ's ambassadors or representatives on earth. **2Corinthians 5:20**

are aliens and strangers to this world. **1Peter 2:11**

are enemies of the devil. **1Peter 5:8**

are sheep cared for by their Shepherd. **Psalm 23; John 10:7-16**

SUMMARY

- God has reconciled people back to Himself.

- God's wrath has been satisfied through the death of Jesus.

- God can forgive sinners of all their sins and declare them righteous.

- God gives believers spiritual life through the indwelling Holy Spirit.

- God offers salvation as a free gift, which can never be lost or stolen.

- God accepts saved persons at the time of salvation.

- Mankind receives salvation through faith alone and not by works.

- Believers grow in their Christian life by grace through faith.

- Believers receive blessings at the time of their salvation.

FOR CONSIDERATION

Allow God to remind you that He is your only Life this week. Thank Him for the fact that He accepts you in Christ. Thank Him also that you do not have to work at it to be accepted by Him. You are righteous, holy and acceptable. You are totally forgiven.

CHAPTER 16
Centrality of The Cross of Christ

Exodus 12:11; Leviticus 17:11; Psalm 103:11-12;
Matthew 6:12-14; Luke 23:34;
John 3:16-17; 8:36; 19:30; Acts 3:26; 4:12;
Romans 4:24-25; 5:8; 6:4-8; 6:12; 8:1; 8:11;
1Corinthians 1:18; 1:23; 2:2; 3:12; 5:4;15:3-4, 21-22;
2 Corinthians 4:14; Galatians 3:1; 5:1; 5:24; 6:14;
Ephesians 1:20; 2:1-3; 2:6; 2:8-10; 4:10: Colossians
1:26-28; 2:12; 2:20; 1Thessalonians 5:10; 5:23-24;
2 Timothy 2:11; Hebrews 12:1-2 (NKJV)

The Centrality of the Cross is a foundational value, encompassing the believer's co-crucifixion, burial, resurrection, ascension and seating with Christ in heaven. This creates a new identity of righteousness and provides a source of power as one appropriates the Life of Christ for daily living.

In the Cross for the sinner, we see a display of God's grace for salvation – **payment of sin's price.**

"For by grace you have been saved through faith; and that not of yourselves, it is the gift of God; not as a result of works, so that no one may boast." **Ephesians 2:8-9**

God's saving grace has changed what direction we are going (towards heaven now). When Jesus said, *"...it is finished..."* **John 19:30**, it truly was. The faith we need to be saved originated with Him and is provided by Him. Apart from the cross, there is no salvation. It is central to being saved. Paul said, *"For the word of the cross is foolishness to those who are perishing, but to us who are being saved it is the power of God."* **1Corinthians 1:18**. He goes on to say, *"And there is salvation in no one* *else; for there is no other Name under heaven that has been given among men by which we must be saved."* **Acts 4:12**

The truth is mankind is born in Adam with a spiritual birth defect. We actually were born with a dead spirit toward God. We were born dead in our sins shaking our fist in God's face while running in the opposite direction. **Romans 5:12, Ephesians 2:1-3**

Yet because of God's unfailing love and unending mercy, He unconditionally pursued us with an all-consuming desire to melt our hearts with Himself. He knew that one day we would bow the knee and confess with our mouth that Jesus Christ is Lord.

"For God so loved the world, that He gave His only begotten Son, that whoever believes in Him shall not perish, but have eternal life. For God did not send the Son into the world to judge the world, but that the world might be saved through Him." **John 3:16-17**

In the Cross for the saint, we see a display of God's grace for sanctification – **for the journey of Life.**

Simply put, sanctification is being set apart. It is being distinguished from others. It is how the believer grows in his/her relationship with Christ. In **1Thessalonians 5:24** we are told that Father God will do it. He is faithful and He will complete the work He has begun. It is based on the nature and character of God. The good news is that it doesn't depend on you or me. As we rest in Christ' finished work on the Cross we can experience His power and presence in our lives in an intimate way. *"Now may the God of peace Himself sanctify you entirely; and may your spirit and soul and body be* *preserved complete, without blame at the coming of our Lord Jesus Christ. Faithful is He who calls you, and He also will bring it to pass."* **1Thessalonians 5:23-24**

He, likewise, sustains living the Christian Life. We don't "try to have faith," or "try to keep our faith." If this is the case, then we are trying by self-effort. That is spelled **S-E-L-F.** It is focusing on oneself instead of Christ. Spell it backwards and add an "H" at the end.

F-L-E-S-H. Any work that is done trusting in our S-E-L-F is done in the flesh, and will be burned up - even good Christian works (i.e. read my bible, have quiet times, go to church, pray). These would be known as "good flesh." They are nothing but wood, hay and stubble **1Corinthians 3:12**. The self-life (one's own efforts) is an individual living from his or her resources and coping mechanisms, which the Bible refers to as walking after the flesh.

A caution must be stated with regard to the flesh. We can become so concerned with the flesh, that we discount ourselves as to not mattering at all. With false humility we can so loathe ourselves to the point of denying our humanity. I call this modern day asceticism. Phrases like "I'm nothing," or "it is all Jesus" etc. can debase someone who Father really cares about… you!

Yes, the bible does say that *"…we are His workmanship, created in Christ Jesus for good works, which God prepared beforehand so that we would walk in them."* **Ephesians 2:10** The phrase "created in Christ Jesus to do good works, "is at times thought by people to mean that we are to do them through our own effort. However, that little big word "in" before Christ Jesus, points to the Initiator and Author of the work: Jesus. It is His Life living in you and through you, not your self-life that produces the work. He is called the *"...Author and Finisher of our faith..."* **Hebrews 12:1-2(NKJV)**

Without the Cross, the Christian is lost - utterly and completely. The centrality of the Cross is not only for salvation, but also sanctification - to live out the Christian Life. We are to depend on Jesus in order to be set apart for all the works He wants to do through us. By faith, we step out and believe that what we are doing is due to His initiation. He has created us to be human. He lives and works through our humanity. He lives and works through our God-given personalities that are wrought with emotions. Emotions are neither good nor bad. They are used for expression - to show those on the outside, what may be happening on the inside of us.

"For God so loved the world, that He gave His only begotten Son, that whoever believes in Him shall not perish, but have eternal life. For God did not send the Son into the world to judge the world, but that the world might be saved through Him." **John 3:16-17**

With the understanding of the centrality of the Cross, we learn to see pain, hurt and injustice through Father's eyes. Our tolerance and bandwidth for compassion and mercy will increase because of His Life in us. We also have a greater appreciation for forgiveness. In **Matthew 6:12-14** we read: *"'And forgive us our debts, as we also have forgiven our debtors. And lead us not into temptation, but deliver us from the evil one. For if you forgive other people when they sin against you, your heavenly Father will also forgive you. But if you do not forgive others their sins, your Father will not forgive your sins.'"*

We first come to Christ to have our sins (past, present and future) forgiven. We're told that Jesus died on the cross for our sins. *"For as high as the heavens are above the earth, So great is His loving-kindness toward those who fear Him. As far as the east is from the west, so far has He removed our transgressions from us."* **Psalm 103:11-12**. He says that He throws our sins in the sea of forgetfulness and remembers them no more... It's not that He has a bad memory. He lovingly chooses to forgive us of our sins. Likewise, we too have a greater capacity to forgive both others and ourselves.

To understand this type of forgiveness is to feel the heart of God. It was the last hour on the Cross before Jesus would die for the sins of the entire world. He is tired and broken emotionally, mentally, and physically. It was in that state of utter helplessness He forgives a sinful man who was next to Him who deserved the punishment due him. Jesus also utters to Father an intercessory prayer for the forgiveness of those who were sinning against Him and for everyone one of us who would be born. He cries out, "...Father, forgive them; for they do not know what they are doing." And they cast lots, dividing up His garments among themselves..." **Luke 23:34**

The cross of Christ is God's heart being spilled out to you saying I forgive you always and promise never to bring it up again. *"It was for freedom that Christ set us free..."* **Galatians 5:1** *"So if the Son makes you free, you will be free indeed."* **John 8:36** As far as condemnation, *"Therefore there is now no condemnation for those who are in Christ Jesus."* **Romans 8:1**

Most believers are familiar with the teaching of the "blood side" of the Cross. We know that the blood of

Christ was spilled for all of our past, present and future sins - we are forgiven.

"For the life of the flesh is in the blood, and I have given it to you on the altar to make atonement for your souls; for it is the blood by reason of the life that makes atonement." **Leviticus 17:11**

The blood of Christ was shed for us - the payment for sin (death) was paid in full.

The "body side" of the cross is for the journey in life. The body side of the cross is generally overlooked or not realized by some Pastors and Christians because they are inadvertently taught that "Now you're saved, try to be a good Christian!" "You need to do your part!" "Honor the gift that God gave you!" As we have already seen, these are statements based on the law.

In the Old Testament, **Exodus 12:11**, shows the specific way that the Israelites were to eat the Passover lamb:
"Now you shall eat it in this manner: with your loins girded, your sandals on your feet, and your staff in your hand; and you shall eat it in haste—it is the LORD'S Passover." They were to be dressed and ready to go. They had a long journey and this event was a picture of walking through this life. Leaving the past life and embarking on the new, committed to never return. In the dark time (night) God would be there to light the way. In the light time (day), Father would be there to guide them, as well. They needed direction in life and Father was there to guide them.

This was a picture of how Christ's body was consumed in order to show that Christ would live in the children of God and would forevermore. He was to be the sustenance for their journey of Life. "The Lamb of God." He was to be their very Life - their only Life. Jesus was and is to live through us. We were never supposed to try and live the Christian Life. It was and is impossible.

The only hope we have of "living the Christian Life" is found in **Colossians 1:26-28** *"that is, the mystery which has been hidden from the past ages and generations, but has now been manifested to His saints, to whom God willed to make known what is the riches of the glory of this mystery among the Gentiles, which is Christ in you, the hope of glory. We proclaim Him, admonishing every man and teaching every man with all wisdom, so that we may present every man complete in Christ."*

In the following table, we see how the blood side and the body side of the Cross reveal that what was true of Jesus, is now true of us as well. We were crucified with Him; we died with Him; we were buried with Him; we were resurrected with Him; we have ascended with Him.

THE CROSS

Blood Side   Body Side

DIED FOR US	DEAD WITH CHRIST
ROM. 5:8 – *"But God demonstrates His own love for us in this: While we were still sinners, Christ died for us."*	**ROM. 6:8** – *"Now if we died with Christ, we believe that we will also live with Him."*
1 THESS. 5:10 – *"He died for us so that, whether we are awake or asleep, we may live together with Him."*	**COL. 2:20** – *"Since you died with Christ to the elemental spiritual forces of this world, why, as though you still belonged to the world, do you submit to its rules?"*
1 COR. 15:3 – *"For what I received I passed on to you as of first importance: that Christ died for our sins according to the Scriptures.*	**2 TIM. 2:11**- *"Here is a trustworthy saying: If we died with Him, we will also live with Him;*
LEV. 17:11 - *"…For the life of a creature is in the blood…*	**LEV. 17:11** - *"…it is the blood that makes atonement for one's life."**

CRUCIFIED FOR US	CRUCIFIED WITH CHRIST
1 COR. 1:23 – *"but we preach Christ crucified: a stumbling block to Jews and foolishness to Gentiles"*	**I AM – GAL. 2:20** – *"I have been crucified with Christ and I no longer live, but Christ lives in me. The life I now live in the body, I live by faith in the Son of God, who loved me and gave Himself for me."*
1 COR. 2:2 – *"For I resolved to know nothing while I was with you except Jesus Christ and Him crucified."*	**OLD MAN – ROM 6:6** – *"For we know that our old self was crucified with Him so that the body ruled by sin might be done away with, that we should no longer be slaves to sin—"*
GAL. 3:1 – *"You foolish Galatians! Who has bewitched you? Before your very eyes Jesus Christ was clearly portrayed as crucified."*	**FLESH – GAL. 5:24** – *"Those who belong to Christ Jesus have crucified the flesh with its passions and desires.* **WORLD – GAL. 6:14** – *"May I never boast except in the cross of our Lord Jesus Christ, through which the world has been crucified to me, and I to the world."*

BURIED ACCORDING TO SCRIPTURE	BURIED WITH HIM
I COR. 15:4 – "*that He was buried, that he was raised on the third day according to the Scriptures,*"	**ROM. 6:4** – "*We were therefore buried with Him through baptism into death in order that, just as Christ was raised from the dead through the glory of the Father, we too may live a new life.*" **COL. 2:12** – "*having been buried with Him in baptism, in which you were also raised with Him through your faith in the working of God, who raised Him from the dead.*"

RESURRECTED FOR US	RESURRECTED WITH HIM
1 COR. 15:4 – *"that He was buried, that He was raised on the third day according to the Scriptures,"* **ROM. 4:24-25** – *"but also for us, to whom God will credit righteousness—for us who believe in Him who raised Jesus our Lord from the dead. He was delivered over to death for our sins and was raised to life for our justification."* **ACTS 3:26** – *"When God raised up His servant, He sent Him first to you to bless you by turning each of you from your wicked ways."* **1 COR. 15:21-22** – *"For since death came through a man, the resurrection of the dead comes also through a man. For as in Adam all die, so in Christ all will be made alive."*	**ROM. 6:4,5,8** – *"We were therefore buried with Him through baptism into death in order that, just as Christ was raised from the dead through the glory of the Father, we too may live a new life. For if we have been united with Him in a death like His, we will certainly also be united with Him in a resurrection like His. Now if we died with Christ, we believe that we will also live with Him."* **ROM. 8:11-** *"And if the Spirit of Him who raised Jesus from the dead is living in you, He who raised Christ from the dead will also give life to your mortal bodies because of His Spirit who lives in you."* **2 COR. 4:14** – *"because we know that the one who raised the Lord Jesus from the dead will also raise us with Jesus and present us with you to Himself."*

ASCENDED TO THE FATHER	ASCENDED AND SEATED WITH HIM
EPH. 1:20 – "*…He raised Christ from the dead and seated Him at His right hand in the heavenly realms*" **EPH. 4:10** – "*He who descended is the very one who ascended higher than all the heavens, in order to fill the whole universe.*"	**EPH. 2:6** – "*And God raised us up with Christ and seated us with Him in the heavenly realms in Christ Jesus,*"

SUMMARY

- God has reconciled people back to Himself.

- God's wrath has been satisfied through the death of Jesus.

- God can forgive sinners of all their sins and declare them righteous.

- Mankind receives salvation through faith alone and not by works.

- Believers grow in their Christian life by grace through faith.

- Believers have been given everything they need for Christian living through their knowledge of God and through the power and presence of Christ as their lives.

- The centrality of the cross of Christ for salvation

- The centrality of the cross of Christ for sanctification (setting apart/living life)

- Without the Cross, the Christian is lost - utterly and completely.

- Jesus blood was shed to forgive all of my sins.

- Jesus body was given to sustain me through this Life.

- Jesus is my only Life.

FOR CONSIDERATION

Allow God to remind you that He is your only Life this week. Thank Him for the fact that because of the centrality of the Cross of Christ, He accepts you completely. Thank Him for His Body that sustains us through this Life. Thank Him for His Blood that has caused you to be completely forgiven. Thank Him also that you are righteous, holy and acceptable to Him and will be forever more.

CHAPTER 17
God Initiates Our Growth In Christ

Ezekiel 36:26-27; John 3:6 15:1-5; Hebrews 12:2;
Romans 5:8; 6; 7:14-20; 8:1-3; 10:9-13; 12:1;
ICorinthians 3:7-8; Galatians 2:20; 5:22-23;
Ephesians 2:6; Philippians 1:6; 2:12-13;
Colossians 3:9; 1Thessalonians 4:13-18;
2Peter 1:3-4; 3:18

It's essential to recognize that God initiates the growth process in a believer's life, just as He initiated His plan of redemption, called sanctification. Just as salvation is received by grace through faith, sanctification also comes by grace through faith. Believers are active in the process of Christian growth and are to work out their salvation:

"So then, my beloved, just as you have always obeyed, not as in my presence only, but now much more in my absence, work out your salvation with fear and trembling; for it is God who is at work in you, both to will and to work for His good pleasure." **Philippians 2:12-13**

How are we to work out our salvation? By realizing that *"it is God who is at work in you, both to will and to work for His good pleasure."* He does it as we rest in Him! What is "our part?" To believe, and even that is initiated and sustained by God. Growing in the grace and knowledge of Christ is first and foremost God's work, which He initiates in each person. Only God knows what is best in order to grow us in Him. In **1Corinthians 3:7-8 (NIV)** we read: *"So neither the one who plants nor the one who waters is anything, but only God, who makes things grow. The one who plants and* *the one who waters have one purpose, and they will each be rewarded according to their own labor."*

It is different with every believer. Through hardship or ease God uses it all *"to work for His good pleasure."* **Philippians 2:13** One thing that a plant needs is fertilizer. Fertilizer stinks, it isn't pleasant, it can burn, it can hurt, etc. But it is needed. As a plant needs three principle things for growth, so do we. We need the Father (Gardener); the Son (Seed) and the Holy Spirit (Water). The grace message is formed in us from "glory to glory." God starts the work in each believer's life and He is faithful to complete it **Philippians 1:6**. He has given every believer all they need *[n3]pertaining to life and godliness."* **2Peter 1:3-4**

These truths should bring relief to the weary believer who is carrying the burden for his own spiritual growth. Many believers mistakenly believe that once they are saved, now God expects them to produce fruit through their own dedication and discipline. Their understanding is that God might give them a boost when the going gets tough, but overall they are on their own.

Many believers are on a life-long mission to prove to God that they are "good Christians." This is an improper focus. God has started the work in us and He alone can produce holiness through His Holy Spirit. **John 15:1-5; Galatians 5:22-23** Believers get to to take their focus off of themselves, place it on God and trust in His working in their lives, to renew and revive them and produce fruit. **Hebrews 12:2**

Apart from Him, we can do nothing that will make any difference or that will last. He is no longer the judge keeping score, as we have erroneously believed. He is fully aware that in you, there is no ability to produce righteousness. **Romans 7:14-20** Rest in the fact that everything that needs to be done, was done by Him.

Appendix B
Summary Of Christian Growth Process

IDENTIFICATION WITH CHRIST
Romans 6:11-14

This important section in Romans lays the foundation of the believer's new life in Christ. These verses explain that the old, unregenerate self that was controlled by Satan dies when a person is saved. The old self is co-crucified with Christ. When you believed in Jesus, your old spirit in Adam was united with Jesus and was nailed to the cross. So at the core of our being, we have been crucified with Christ. **Galatians 2:20** We have been co-raised with Jesus, we're new creations and the indwelling Christ is our power and our Life! **John 3:6; Romans 6:5**

Ephesians 2:6 The old man was crucified with Christ **Romans 6:6** and replaced by the new man **Colossians 3:9**. God's Holy Spirit comes to indwell in each person at the time of his or her time of initial salvation. The Holy Spirit can now overcome sin in a person's life, whereas prior to salvation Satan enslaves a person with no hope of true change. As we experience Christ's as Life, we become more aware of who we truly are.

True change comes when the old person is done away with or "exchanged" for the new person we are in Christ. We died with Christ and we are resurrected a new creation in Christ.

Now our spirit is joined to His Spirit. By this union with Christ, we can enjoy living from His Life, which enables us to overcome sin and live righteously. There is a new desire within the person to know God and follow His ways. We are no longer sinners so we cannot sin! In **Romans 5:8** *"But God demonstrates His own love toward us, in that while we were yet sinners, Christ died for us..."* "Were," past tense, meaning that we no longer are. We might ask "but I still do sin, don't I?" Are you saying I don't, when I know that I do?" Let's see what God says.

In **Romans 8:1-3** we read: *"Therefore there is now no condemnation for those who are in Christ Jesus. For the law of the Spirit of life in Christ Jesus has set you free from the law of sin and of death. For what the Law could not do, weak as it was through the flesh, God did: sending His own Son in the likeness of sinful flesh and as an offering for sin, He condemned sin in the flesh..."*

At the core of your being, you are not a sinner but a saint! If you were a sinner, God could not live in you. His Holy Spirit is one with your new spirit.

Also, In **Romans 7:14-18** we read *"For we know that the Law is spiritual, but I am of flesh, sold into bondage to sin. For what I am doing, I do not understand; for I am not practicing what I would like to do, but I am doing the very thing I hate. But if I do the very thing I do not want to do, I agree with the Law, confessing that the Law is good. So now, no longer am I the one doing it, but sin which dwells in me. For I know that nothing good dwells in me, that is, in my flesh; for the willing is present in me, but the doing of the good is not."*

It is the power of sin that is sinning and it is contained in a place called my "flesh." *"So now, no longer am I the one doing it, but sin which dwells in me."* Who I truly am (my completely new spirit) cannot sin. It is impossible! If we give way to the flesh, *"no longer am I the one doing it, but sin which dwells in me, "that is, in my flesh."* The physical body has not been replaced with our new body, yet.

In **2Corinthians 5:1-5(NIV)** we read: *"For we know that if the earthly tent [body] which is our house is torn down, we have a building from God, a house [body] not made with hands, eternal in the heavens. For indeed in this house we groan, longing to be clothed with our dwelling from heaven, inasmuch as we, having put it on, will not be found naked. For indeed while we are in this tent [body], we groan, being burdened, because we do not want to be unclothed but to be clothed, so that what is mortal [body] will be swallowed up by life. Now He who prepared us for this very purpose is God, who gave to us the Spirit as a pledge."*

One day, our spirit will be contained in a new and eternal body. The inside will match the outside. Are we going to believe how we *feel, see or think* or are we going to believe what God says is true about us? For example let me illustrate with an explanation and the diagram below.

How do I trust Christ in believing the truth that I am no longer a sinner but a saint? I can react on my feelings (they are neither good nor bad). If I base them on a false belief (I don't feel holy), then in my mind I act on that false belief and I will do what I believe is true (which isn't) and the result will be that I don't believe when God says I am holy.

However, if I am presented with the same truth and I believe (with my mind of Christ) that I am holy (The Holy Spirit reveals it to me), then I do believe what Father says about me (that I am holy) regardless of how I feel. I then believe the truth and my emotions may or may not align with the Truth. I believe what Father says is true regardless of how I think or feel.

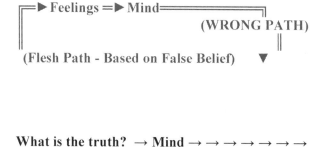

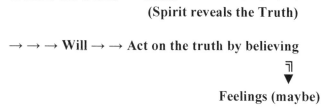

CHAPTER 18
THE SPIRIT-FILLED LIFE

Genesis 15:6; Deuteronomy 31:6; Jeremiah 31;
Ezekiel 36:24-27; Matthew 11:28-30; 13:38-39;
John 1:14; 14:6; 16:33; Romans 5:1-2; 6:1-14; 7:7-25;
Romans 8:1-11; 1Corinthians 3:16; 7:5; 15:10;
2Corinthians 2:10-11; 5:21; 1Timothy 3;
Galatians 2:20; 3:1-5; 5:16-25; 1John 4:4;
Ephesians 2:14-15; 3:19-20; 4:6; 5:18; 6:10-18;
Philippians 1:6; 2:12-13; 3:9-14; James 4:7;
Colossians 1:25-29; 2:1-15; 3:1-4; Titus 1:5-9;
Hebrews 5:7-9; 8:13; 1Peter 5:8; 2Peter 1:3;

At the time of salvation, all believers have their old
selves crucified with Christ, **Romans 6:1-14** and receive
the Holy Spirit. **Romans 8:9; 1Corinthians 3:16**
However, not all believers experience the Spirit-filled
life. Since Paul felt the need to command believers to be
filled with the Spirit in **Ephesians 5:18.** Being filled
with the Spirit should not be confused with the coming
of the Spirit in **Acts 2.** Someone should not expect
speaking in tongues or other dramatic experiences as the
sign of being filled with the Spirit.

The Holy Spirit is just as fully present in a new believer,
a mature believer or a carnal believer. The issue is
whether someone is surrendering to the Spirit.
Surrendering to the Spirit is a submitting oneself to His
will rather than doing the will of our flesh. It's deciding
to turn from the flesh by relying on God's power and
grace and allowing the Spirit to work freely as your life.
The Spirit is fully inside of each believer but He can be
quenched through a failure to surrender to Him. Our
focus should not be on trying to get more of the Spirit in
us, but recognizing that God has already placed His

Spirit in us. We can choose to simply surrender to Him to bring forth the Spirit's work and fruit in our lives. Since the fruit of the Spirit is love, joy, peace, patience, etc. **Galatians 5:22-23,** these qualities in a person's life are the genuine evidences of the Holy Spirit, not dramatic experiences.

The Scriptures also speak of Christ, **Galatians 2:20,** and the Father, **Ephesians 3:19-20; 4:6**, Himself as indwelling believers. This shows us that all three persons of the Trinity indwell believers. Before the New Covenant, God resided in the temple, separated from His people. It is both amazing and humbling to consider that God, in all of His fullness, now resides in each believer. To reside in someone that He created, is miraculous! It is something that only God could do.

This is important because Christians often mistakenly think of the Spirit as a force that empowers them, rather than as a Person that indwells them and lives as Life through them. Paul was aware that Christ, by His Spirit, lived in him and he spoke of living his life as evidenced by **Galatians 2:20** *"I have been crucified with Christ; and it is no longer I who live, but Christ lives in me; and the life which I now live in the flesh I live by faith in the Son of God, who loved me and gave Himself up for me."* Paul was convinced that he could not live righteously, **Romans 7:7-25**, nor produce fruit. By this, he knew that Christ lived in him and He could produce the fruit of the Spirit as evidence of Jesus being his life. So he lived his life by faith in the indwelling Christ and not in himself.

This has been described as living the "Exchanged Life", since the believer has had his unrighteousness "exchanged" for Christ's righteousness and his old life "exchanged" for Christ as his only Life. **Romans 6:4** confirms this: *"Therefore we have been buried with Him through baptism into death, so that as Christ was raised from the dead through the glory of the Father, so we too might walk in newness of life."* Out with the old, in with the new!

Believers have Paul's example, whose trust was in Jesus and not in himself, to live the Christian life. It is not difficult to live the "Christian Life," it is IMPOSSIBLE! Only one person has lived the "Christian Life" perfectly... Jesus. Understanding this truth can relieve Christians of the burden of trying to be righteous in themselves. Once again, we see that the glory goes to God, since He alone can produce righteousness in and through His children as they surrender to Him. Father wants to reveal Himself through all of us. Will you let Him live through you? If so, how is this done? How does the Person and work of the Holy Spirit make a difference in our life?

Not only will we have the Father and Son in us but also another Advocate. Jesus says that the Holy Spirit will come into us when we are saved. He is the Spirit of all Truth. We will know Him because He is living in us forever! Jesus says that He is not leaving us as orphans. We won't be left without guidance. The Holy Spirit will reveal Jesus to us. Jesus is the Truth. *"If you love Me, keep My commands. And I will ask the Father, and He will give you another Advocate to help you and be with you forever - the Spirit of Truth. The world cannot accept Him, because it neither sees Him nor knows Him. But you know Him, for He lives with you and will be in you. I will not leave you as orphans; I will come to you."*
John 4:15-18(NIV)

He will speak to us: *"While they were ministering to the Lord and fasting, the Holy Spirit said, 'Set apart for Me Barnabas and Saul for the work to which I have called them.'"* **Acts 13:2**

The Holy Spirit will comfort us. He will give us the peace of being in Jesus. *"These things I have spoken to you while abiding with you. But the Helper, the Holy Spirit, whom the Father will send in My name, He will teach you all things, and bring to your remembrance all that I said to you. Peace I leave with you; My peace I give to you; not as the world gives do I give to you. Do not let your heart be troubled, nor let it be fearful.'"* **John 14:25-27**

The Holy Spirit directs us *"Be on guard for yourselves and for all the flock, among which the Holy Spirit has made you overseers, to shepherd the church of God which He purchased with His own blood."* **Acts 20:28**
The Holy Spirit confirms things in our conscience *"I am telling the truth in Christ, I am not lying, my conscience testifies with me in the Holy Spirit."* **Romans 9:1**

The Holy Spirit is our power *"Now may the God of hope fill you with all joy and peace in believing, so that you will abound in hope by the power of the Holy Spirit."* **Romans 15:13**

We were reborn and received our new spirit through Him *"He saved us, not on the basis of deeds which we have done in righteousness, but according to His mercy, by the washing of regeneration and renewing by the Holy Spirit."* **Titus 3:5**

The Holy Spirit also gives spiritual gifts as He determines to. *"Now there are varieties of gifts, but the same Spirit. And there are varieties of ministries, and the same Lord. There are varieties of effects, but the same God who works all things in all persons. But to each one is given the manifestation of the Spirit for the common good. For to one is given the word of wisdom through the Spirit, and to another the word of knowledge according to the same Spirit; to another faith by the same Spirit, and to another gifts of healing by the one Spirit, and to another the effecting of miracles, and to another prophecy, and to another the distinguishing of spirits, to another various kinds of tongues, and to another the interpretation of tongues. But one and the same Spirit works all these things, distributing to each one individually just as He wills.* **1Corinthians 12:4-11**

Lastly, *"In Him, you also, after listening to the message of truth, the gospel of your salvation having also believed, you were sealed in Him with the Holy Spirit of promise."* **Ephesians 1:13**

The deal is done! It can never be undone! You and I have been marked with the seal of approval - the Holy Spirit.

VICTORY OVER SATAN
Ephesians 6:10-18; James 4:7

"For our struggle is not against flesh and blood, but against the rulers, against the powers, against the world forces of this darkness, against the spiritual forces of wickedness in the heavenly places." **Ephesians 6:12** Although there is a struggle for the believer with his flesh on a daily basis, in this verse, Paul boldly states that the struggle to live righteously is ultimately a battle against Satan and his demons.

Ever since their rebellion against God, the demons have actively worked against God and against people. Satan works to keep both unbelievers and believers from knowing God and His Truth. One of his most effective lies is to convince Christians that he (Satan) does not exist or at least that he is not actively working against all believers. Christians need to be convinced that Satan is indeed alive and is constantly trying to tempt believers and trying to lure them away from God and His truth. **Matthew 13:38-39; 1Corinthians 7:5; 2Corinthians 2:10-11; 1Peter 5:8** However, Christ has already triumphed over Satan. **Colossians 2:9-15; 1John 4:4** Through resting in Christ as life and strength, all believers can experience victory over Satan!

A key word used several times in **Ephesians 6:10-18** is "stand". Believers are exhorted to stand their ground against the devil's schemes. This is because God has already placed the believer in a secure position. Satan cannot change the fact that a believer is forgiven; declared and made righteous in God's sight; reconciled back to God; has God's Spirit living in him; will spend eternity with God, etc.

But Satan can deceive us with lies, which may cause us to doubt God's Truth and draw our focus off of our secure relationship with God and onto our failures, doubts, and sins, etc. Believers can feel powerless simply through believing Satan's lies and deceptions. That is why in **Ephesians 6:14-18,** Paul urges believers to stand firm in the armor of God, which He has provided for our protection. Studying these verses can give insight into the spiritual battle against Satan.

James' message is simple: submit to God, resist the devil and he will flee. The believer is to actively stand against

Satan and resist him, but it is imperative that he stands strong in God's armor **Ephesians 6:13** and submits to God as in **James 4:7.**

In **Ephesians 6:14-18(NIV)** we read about the Armor of God: "*Stand firm then, with the belt of truth buckled around your waist,*" Jesus is the Truth, **John 14:6** "*with the breastplate of righteousness in place,*" Jesus is our righteousness **2Corinthians 5:21**, "*and with your feet fitted with the readiness that comes from the gospel of peace,*" Jesus is our peace, **Ephesians 2:14-15**, "*In addition to all this, take up the shield of faith,*" Jesus is our faith, **Romans 5:1-2**, "*with which you can extinguish all the flaming arrows of the evil one.*" "*Take the helmet of salvation,*" Jesus is our salvation, **Hebrews 5:7-9**, "*and the sword of the Spirit, which is the word of God,*" Jesus is the Word of God, **John 1:14**, "*And pray in the Spirit on all occasions with all kinds of prayers and requests. With this in mind, be alert and always keep on praying for all the Lord's people.*" In other words, realize that you are clothed in Jesus - He is the Armor of God! He has said He will "*never leave you nor forsake you*" **Deuteronomy 31:6**

Grace Maturity and Leaders

Paul lists the characteristics of grace maturity for elders, deacons and deaconesses in these passages. These qualities and life patterns emerge as a result of the indwelling Spirit manifesting Himself through the yielded life of a believer. Paul was instructing Timothy and Titus to look for these characteristics because they were evidence of the Holy Spirit in an individual God was preparing for a leadership role.

"It is a trustworthy statement: if any man aspires to the office of overseer, it is a fine work he desires to do. An overseer, then, must be above reproach, the husband of one wife, temperate, prudent, respectable, hospitable, able to teach, not addicted to wine or pugnacious, but gentle, peaceable, free from the love of money. He must be one who manages his own household well, keeping his children under control with all dignity (but if a man does not know how to manage his own household, how will he take care of the church of God?), and not a new convert, so that he will not become conceited and fall into the condemnation incurred by the devil. And he must have a good reputation with those outside the church, so that he will not fall into reproach and the snare of the devil.

Deacons likewise must be men of dignity, not double-tongued, or addicted to much wine or fond of sordid gain, but holding to the mystery of the faith with a clear conscience. These men must also first be tested; then let them serve as deacons if they are beyond reproach.
Women must likewise be dignified, not malicious gossips, but temperate, faithful in all things. Deacons must be husbands of only one wife, and good managers of their children and their own households. For those who have served well as deacons obtain for themselves a high standing and great confidence in the faith that is in Christ Jesus." **1Timothy 3:1-13**

"For this reason I left you in Crete, that you would set in order what remains and appoint elders in every city as I directed you, namely, if any man is above reproach, the husband of one wife, having children who believe, not accused of dissipation or rebellion. For the overseer must be above reproach as God's steward, not self-willed, not quick-tempered, not addicted to wine, not

pugnacious, not fond of sordid gain, but hospitable, loving what is good, sensible, just, devout, self-controlled, holding fast the faithful word which is in accordance with the teaching, so that he will be able both to exhort in sound doctrine and to refute those who contradict." **Titus 1:5-9**

There are several areas that stand out as flowing consistently with the previous chapters. Justification comes through faith, not by works of any kind. This is consistent with God's Grace as seen throughout the Bible. **Genesis 15:6** Believers are secure in their salvation, which is consistent with God providing salvation as a gift throughout the Bible. The glorious New Covenant, which was promised in **Jeremiah 31**, has now begun, replacing the Old Covenant and rendering it obsolete. **Hebrews 8:13** Just as God has taken the initiative towards man for salvation, He also takes the initiative in beginning the process of growth in each believer and continuing the growth process to its completion **Philippians 1:6**

Throughout the Bible, man's sinful actions show that he has a sinful, evil heart prior to salvation. Apart from God transferring man from the achieving system, in Adam, to the receiving system, in Christ, there is no hope for a new life marked by obedience. It's the difference between being driven by the flesh versus being drawn by the Spirit. In **Ezekiel 36:24-27**, God promised to give people a new heart and a new spirit. God fulfilled His promise by sending His Spirit to live inside of all believers. He exchanged the old dead heart and spirit, for a new living heart and spirit.

SUMMARY

- God has reconciled people back to Himself.

- God's wrath has been satisfied through the death of Jesus.

- God can forgive sinners of all their sins and declare them righteous
  .

- God gives believers spiritual life through the indwelling Holy Spirit.

- God offers salvation as a free gift, which can never be lost or stolen.

- Unsaved man receives salvation through faith alone and not by works.

- Believers grow in their Christian life by grace through faith.

- Believers have everything they need for Christian living through their knowledge of God and through the power and presence of Christ as their lives.

- Believers can stand firm against Satan.

- Believers have been given every spiritual blessing in Christ.

FOR CONSIDERATION

Allow God to remind you that He is your Life this week by repeating and meditating on all the spiritual blessings you have as a believer in Christ.

CHAPTER 19
Jesus Returns for His People

1Timothy 4; 2Timothy 3:1-5; 2Peter 3:3-10;
1Corinthians 15:51-52; 1Thessalonians 4:13-18;
Matthew 16:18; 24:3-31; 24:36-44; 25:31-46;
Revelation 19:1-18; 20:1-10; 6-1620:11-15; 21:1-27;
Revelation 22:3-21;4:8-11; 5:9-14; 11:15-18; 12:10-12;
Revelation 15:3-4;19:1-9; John 3:17; Titus 2:13

When Jesus came to this earth over 2,000 years ago, He came to save the world, not to judge it; *"For God did not send the Son into the world to judge the world, but that the world might be saved through Him."* **John 3:17**. After Jesus ascended, His Holy Spirit came to live inside of Jesus' followers on the Day of Pentecost. Since that day, Jesus has been building His church worldwide through the lives of His disciples. **Matthew 16:18** Meanwhile, Satan has been actively advancing his own kingdom by blinding unbelievers from God's truth and by blinding believers to the truth of Christ as Life. However, Jesus promised that He would come again to the earth. Next time He will judge all people and bind up Satan for a period of time.

"Then I saw an angel coming down from heaven, holding the key of the abyss and a great chain in his hand. And he laid hold of the dragon, the serpent of old, who is the devil and Satan, and bound him for a thousand years; and he threw him into the abyss, and shut it and sealed it over him, so that he would not deceive the nations any longer, until the thousand years were completed; after these things he must be released for a short time." **Revelation 20:1-3**

Ultimately, Jesus will cast Satan into hell and set things right. This chapter surveys the final events in Jesus' Second Coming and the believer's future heavenly home. The premillennial, pre-tribulation view is presented here.

There are different views as to when Jesus will return. There's the Premillennial view - Jesus coming back before the millennial (1000 year reign) Kingdom is established and to establish it both physically and spiritually; the Postmillennial position - Jesus comes back at the end of the 1000 years and judges the world; and the Amillennial view that believes that the 1000 year reign is symbolic in nature and that the millennium has already begun and is actually the current church age. There can be a lot of "hype" with regard to the return of Jesus. Is it pre- post- amil or some other millennial view? The important thing is that you are saved and there is no need to worry when Jesus will return. He will return and that is what is most important!

Although there are several passages describing the end times, the Bible does not specify the time of the great event, the Rapture. It could occur at any moment. During the Rapture, Jesus will come down from heaven with the spirits of believers who have already died. All believers who are living on earth at that moment will physically rise up into the air to meet the Lord Jesus. They will all be changed in an instant and given new resurrection bodies. This glorious coming of Jesus for His own is the "blessed hope" of all believers. **Titus 2:13** Jesus and His children will then remain in heaven until the millennial period.

One might think that finally all unbelievers will believe! Not necessarily. Satan will continue to have a strong deceptive influence on the unsaved. With all the "aliens this" and "aliens that," one couldn't help but think he'd say that aliens or some other ridiculous excuse abducted them. Nonetheless, the Rapture will happen and it is a biblical certainty.

Following the Rapture, all those remaining on the earth will face a horrible 7-year period called the Tribulation. Jesus described it like this, *"For then there will be a great tribulation, such as has not occurred since the beginning of the world until now, nor ever will."* **Matthew 24:21** During the Tribulation, Satan will use a powerful person, the Anti-Christ, to gain world control and to deceive most people away from God's truth. God will pour out His wrath upon unbelievers and many will die. However, a small percentage of people will believe in Jesus and be saved.

At the end of the Tribulation, Jesus will come again to the earth, bringing with Him all resurrected believers. This is His Second Coming. He will come with power and glory and defeat Satan in the great Battle of Armageddon. **Revelation 16:16** He will judge both Jewish people and Gentiles (non-Jewish persons) and will also bind Satan for 1,000 years. As already mentioned, this period of 1,000 years is called the Millennium or Millennial Kingdom. Christ will rule the earth during this period of peace when many will come to faith in Him, including many Jewish people.

At the end of the 1,000 years, Satan will be released for a short time and allowed to deceive many. God will then crush Satan's rebellion and cast him into the Lake of Fire where he will be "[10]...they will be tormented day and night forever and ever." **Revelation 20:10** The Great White Throne Judgment follows in which all unbelievers, those whose names were not found written in the Lamb's Book of Life, are justly condemned and cast into the Lake of Fire for eternal punishment. **Revelation13:8; 21:27**

Even now, unbelievers benefit from the blessings of God though they do not acknowledge Him as Lord and Savior of their lives. They experience the goodness of God, yet they do not know Him. Imagine living for all eternity with no blessings at all. To be eternally separated from God - the Blesser of our lives.

God will then create a new heaven and a new earth where He will reign over His people throughout all eternity: *"And I heard a loud voice from the throne, saying, "Behold, the tabernacle of God is among men, and He will dwell among them, and they shall be His people, and God Himself will be among them, and He will wipe away every tear from their eyes; and there will no longer be any death; there will no longer be any mourning, or crying, or pain; the first things have passed away."* **Revelation 20:3-4**

God's glorious plan to bring His people back to Him is now complete! The barrier and separation between man and God that began in the Garden of Eden has been removed through the sacrifice of the *"Lamb who has been slain."* **Revelation 13:8** Only God could have the wisdom, love and grace to devise and carry out such a plan. All who trust in Jesus alone for their salvation are the recipients of His lavish grace.

Jesus will defeat Satan and his armies. **Revelation 19:11-21** He will then ultimately judge Satan and send him into the Lake of Fire for eternal punishment. **Revelation 20:10** Unbelievers will be judged at the Great White Throne and sent into the Lake of Fire. **Revelation 20:11-15**

Revelation 4:8 describes creatures in heaven who day and night never stop saying: *"HOLY, HOLY, HOLY is THE LORD GOD, THE ALMIGHTY, WHO WAS AND WHO IS AND WHO IS TO COME."* God's holiness, righteousness and justice are proclaimed in **Revelation 15:3-4; 16:5-7. Revelation 9:15-16; 14:17-20** and other passages, describe God's wrath on unbelievers, resulting in physical death and eternal punishment.

2Peter3:9 describes God's gracious patience: *"[He] is patient toward you, not wishing for any to perish but for all to come to repentance."* After the rapture, all people still on the earth who have not yet died, will be given an opportunity to hear the Gospel and be saved. **Matthew 24:14; Revelation 14:6-7** Sadly, despite the horrors of the Tribulation, most people will not repent and turn to God. **Revelation 9:20-21** They will reject God's free offer of eternal life. **Revelation 22:17**

Jesus will bind Satan and rule the earth in peace during this period. This millennial kingdom is described throughout the Old Testament and is the kingdom that Jesus' 12 disciples anticipated. In God's plan this kingdom did not occur during Jesus' first appearance but will occur during His future Second Coming.

God will create a new heaven and earth, with no more death, mourning or pain and will rule His people for eternity. **Revelation 21 - 22** describes the believer's wonderful future heavenly home.

Believers who are living at the time preceding the Rapture will be raptured into the air to meet the Lord. **1Thessalonians 4:13-18; 1Corinthians 15:51-52** describe this future event that could occur at any time. Believers will actually physically rise to meet the Lord in the air and be spared the horrors of the Tribulation. We can only speculate as to how God will bring this about with respect to people being inside buildings, etc. The world will experience a terrible period of tribulation. The passages in Matthew and Revelation vividly describe this time of unprecedented tribulation.

Unbelievers will be judged at the Great White Throne and sent into the Lake of Fire. **Revelation 20:11-15** The Bible is clear and certain about God's judgment and the reality of an eternal hell. Jesus specifically stated in the Gospels regarding hell that it was prepared for the devil and his angels. He never intended hell to be for people made in the image of God.

Revelation 21-22 describes the believer's wonderful future home. God's care is described as very personal and tender, like a loving Shepherd.

Verses 3-7 seem to describe the prevalent attitude in today's society of apathy and unbelief. With so many so-called "prophets" predicting the return of Christ and then being wrong, we know that they are false prophets. A prophet of God is never wrong. More and more as this happens, many will become more and more apathetic. *"and saying, 'Where is the promise of His coming? For ever since the fathers fell asleep, all continues just as it was from the beginning of creation.'"* **2Peter 3:4**

"Know this first of all, that in the last days mockers will come with their mocking, following after their own lusts, and saying, "Where is the promise of His coming? For ever since the fathers fell asleep, all continues just as it was from the beginning of creation." For when they maintain this, it escapes their notice that by the word of

God the heavens existed long ago and the earth was formed out of water and by water, through which the world at that time was destroyed, being flooded with water. But by His word the present heavens and earth are being reserved for fire, kept for the Day of Judgment and destruction of ungodly men.

But do not let this one fact escape your notice, beloved, that with the Lord one day is like a thousand years, and a thousand years like one day. The Lord is not slow about His promise, as some count slowness, but is patient toward you, not wishing for any to perish but for all to come to repentance. But the day of the Lord will come like a thief, in which the heavens will pass away with a roar and the elements will be destroyed with intense heat, and the earth and its works will be burned up.

Since all these things are to be destroyed in this way, what sort of people ought you to be in holy conduct and godliness, looking for and hastening the coming of the day of God, because of which the heavens will be destroyed by burning, and the elements will melt with intense heat! But according to His promise we are looking for new heavens and a new earth, in which righteousness dwells.

Therefore, beloved, since you look for these things, be diligent to be found by Him in peace, spotless and blameless, and regard the patience of our Lord as salvation; just as also our beloved brother Paul, according to the wisdom given him, wrote to you, as also in all his letters, speaking in them of these things, in which are some things hard to understand, which the untaught and unstable distort, as they do also the rest of the Scriptures, to their own destruction. You therefore, beloved, knowing this beforehand, be on your guard so that you are not carried away by the error of unprincipled men and fall from your own steadfastness, but grow in the grace and knowledge of our Lord and Savior Jesus Christ. To Him be the glory, both now and to the day of eternity. Amen." **2Peter 3:3-18**

Verses 8-9 show God's tremendous patience and desire for all to be saved.

Verse 10 *"But the day of the Lord will come like a thief, in which the heavens will pass away with a roar and the elements will be destroyed with intense heat, and the earth and its works will be burned up."* Those who are more closely tied to the things of the world may feel grief of loss of the things they had or could have at that time.

1John 2:15-17 *"Do not love the world or anything in the world. If anyone loves the world, love for the Father is not in them. For everything in the world—the lust of the flesh, the lust of the eyes, and the pride of life—comes not from the Father but from the world. The world and its desires pass away, but whoever does the will of God lives forever. "* What is the will of God? To believe in Him whom He sent - Jesus.

Those who aren't sure that they are saved might feel scared. Those who are sure of their salvation, quite frankly, are looking forward to leaving this existence and may be ecstatic. The future destruction of this earth should motivate believers to lay up treasures in heaven, not on earth;

"Do not store up for yourselves treasures on earth, where moth and rust destroy, and where thieves break in

and steal. But store up for yourselves treasures in heaven, where neither moth nor rust destroys, and where thieves do not break in or steal; for where your treasure is, there your heart will be also." **Matthew 6:19-21**

Nonetheless, to see the big picture will help, in general, believers to sense the deep and enduring love of the Father, Son and Holy Spirit for His children. The storms of this world/life will be more easily tolerated. We know the end of the story and it ends and begins in total victory - one of the many reasons to worship our God for all of eternity. The glory of the Lord will take all of eternity to behold. We will forever be awestruck by our God and Father and the Lord Jesus Christ.

In **Revelation 19:6-9**, we read about the marriage of the Lamb - Jesus. *"Then I heard something like the voice of a great multitude and like the sound of many waters and like the sound of mighty peals of thunder, saying, 'Hallelujah! For the Lord our God, the Almighty, reigns. Let us rejoice and be glad and give the glory to Him, for the marriage of the Lamb has come and His bride has made herself ready.' It was given to her to clothe herself in fine linen, bright and clean; for the fine linen is the righteous acts of the saints. Then he said to me, 'Write, Blessed are those who are invited to the marriage supper of the Lamb.' And he said to me, 'These are true words of God.'"*

Apart from the Cross of Christ (Chapter 16), none of this would be possible. In a marriage ceremony, the bride is the star attraction. She wears a white wedding gown signifying that she is a virgin - that she is pure through and through. In the marriage of the Lamb, it says *"Let us rejoice and be glad and give the glory to Him, for the marriage of the Lamb has come and His bride has made herself ready. It was given to her to clothe herself in fine linen, bright and clean; for the fine linen is the righteous acts of the saints."*

The bride is the church (saints). The church has made herself ready. She is wearing "*...fine linen, bright and clean...* " This was not a dress that she chose; it was given to her to wear. The death of Jesus and all of the saints (you and me) on the cross has made us a new creation. Our spirit is exchanged for a new and pure one. Her purity radiates with brightness and cleanliness. There is no impurity found in her. The centrality of the Cross of Christ is the foundation of the wedding of the Lamb. It was made possible by the Groom. He gave His life for her.

"Husbands, love your wives, just as Christ also loved the church and gave Himself up for her, so that He might sanctify her, having cleansed her by the washing of water with the word, that He might present to Himself the church in all her glory, having no spot or wrinkle or any such thing; but that she would be holy and blameless." **Ephesians 5:25-27**

The Groom gave His life. In so doing, He made it possible for her to be a pure bride," *having no spot or wrinkle or any such thing...Then one of the seven angels who had the seven bowls full of the seven last plagues came and spoke with me, saying, 'Come here, I will show you the bride, the wife of the Lamb.' And he carried me away in the Spirit to a great and high mountain, and showed me the holy city, Jerusalem, coming down out of heaven from God, having the glory of God. Her brilliance was like a very costly stone, as a stone of crystal-clear jasper."* **Revelation 21:9-11**

The consummation of this marriage will result in an intimacy so strong and intimate, that nothing can destroy it! *"The LORD is the one who goes ahead of you; He will be with you. He will not fail you or forsake you. Do not fear or be dismayed."* **Deuteronomy 31:8** Jesus has gone before us and prepared everything for the wedding - even the bride! The point is that He is coming back for His beautiful bride.

The bond between them is so intimate, that it is the closest you can become without being the other person! This marriage to Jesus will be different than even the best Christian marriage possible on this earth! Jesus has made His bride to be radiant - *"as a stone of crystal-clear jasper"*

There is a oneness between the two individuals, that was intended from the beginning of creation. We will be in union for all of eternity! *"But from the beginning of creation, God MADE THEM MALE AND FEMALE. FOR THIS REASON A MAN SHALL LEAVE HIS FATHER AND MOTHER, AND THE TWO SHALL BECOME ONE FLESH; so they are no longer two, but one flesh. What therefore God has joined together, let no man separate."* **Mark 10:6-9**

From the beginning of creation until the marriage of the Lamb, the bride has been prepared. Things will finally be set aright. The marriage celebration will go on forever and ever. We will worship our Groom, with these words, both now and throughout eternity: *"...HOLY, HOLY, HOLY is THE LORD GOD, THE ALMIGHTY, WHO WAS AND WHO IS AND WHO IS TO COME. Worthy are You, our Lord and our God, to receive glory and honor and power; for You created all things, and because of Your will they existed, and were created.'"*

SUMMARY

- Jesus will come again to defeat Satan and judge all unbelievers once and for all.

- Jesus will rule over this present earth for 1,000 years.

- God will create a new heaven and earth, with no more death, mourning or pain and will rule His people for eternity.

- Believers who are living at the time will be raptured into the air to meet the Lord.

- All unbelievers will be judged and cast into the Lake of Fire for eternal punishment. You either know Him in close relationship or you don't. To not, has eternal consequences based solely on your decision.

- Believers will serve God and be comforted by Him throughout eternity.

FOR CONSIDERATION

Allow God to remind you that He is your only Life this week by reflecting on Jesus' ultimate defeat of Satan, judgment of all sin and His tender care for believers in heaven.

Appendix A
Indwelling Sin
AELM Conference Material

God in Christ first replaced our dead spirit ith Christ's Living Spirit. Our soul is transformed moment by moment by the renewing of our mind by replacing lies we believe with the truth of God's Word. When Christ comes again we will experience replacing our old body with a new one. That plays an important role in how that imperfect body works during our time on earth.

Paul tells us in **Romans 7** that we have this "sin that indwells us." This sin is a noun and it is a principle or a power in me, but is not me, however it feels like me. It is similar to having a thorn in your foot. It is in your foot, but it is not your foot. It hurts you, bothers you and impacts you and you know its there, but it is not you. That is what indwelling sin is like. It is in me, in the members of my body, but it is not me. It is important to remember that our true identity is in our spirit. The bible says that we will not get a new body until Jesus' second coming; therefore the indwelling sin will be in us until we get our new resurrected body.

So for now we get to live with this indwelling sin daily. Unfortunately the inner conflict that Paul talks about in Romans is not the flesh. Instead it is an entity all its own that indwells us and appeals to our flesh. Flesh carries out the temptation of the indwelling sin.

We have learned that we are holy, righteous and blameless. Therefore the sinful thoughts that we may struggle with off and on are not ours. According to Paul's example in Romans 7 they are served up in our minds from the principle of sin and appeals to our flesh. Because our indwelling sin has been around for so long and knows our flesh patterns, indwelling sin makes an appeal to our flesh. At that moment in Christ we have a choice to either go with our flesh or surrender to our spirit.

Our new identity tells us who we have now become. Victory in tells us where in Christ we get the power to choose to access His ability or resources to live it out. This is not a ritual a formula some religious achievement on our part that we manage to pull off. Victory is a person! Jesus Christ Himself! He is not a hired holy helper to us; He is our very source of Life!

Paul explains in **Romans 8:2** that *"For the law of the Spirit of life in Christ Jesus has set you free from the law of sin and of death."* When we sin it is our way to meet our legitimate needs in illegitimate ways. To understand that Christ living in me meets all of those needs we really don't have to sin anymore. We are now free from having to depend upon our flesh to get our needs met. In Christ we already have the victory over the sin that indwells us.

In **Romans 6:6** we read, *"knowing this, that our old self was crucified with Him, in order that our body of sin might be done away with, so that we would no longer be slaves to sin."* **Romans 6:11-12** says, *"Even so consider yourselves to be dead to sin, but alive to God in Christ Jesus. Therefore do not let sin reign in your mortal body so that you obey its lusts."*

Appendix B
Summary Of Christian Growth Process

One can see that throughout the Bible God has provided salvation for all people. Man's choice is to accept or reject God's provision. The same is true in the process of Christian growth. God has provided everything needed for believers to grow in holiness *"seeing that His divine power has granted to us everything pertaining to life and godliness, through the true knowledge of Him who called us by His own glory and excellence."* **2Peter 1:3** The believer's choice is to accept God's provision through trusting, surrendering and submitting; or to reject God's provision and live independently of Him.

The believer, who chooses to live independently of God, either through rebellion or through a determination to be holy through his own efforts (the flesh), will always fail to produce the genuine fruit of the Spirit. However, the believer who realizes his own inability to be holy and instead lives in dependence upon the Life of Christ to produce fruit through the believer will experience growing amounts of love, joy, peace righteousness, etc. flowing through him.

Believers are to be active in this process of spiritual growth, but always with the full realization that it is God who initiates and continues His work in each believer and who can give to His children both the desire and ability to carry out His will. That is Paul's message in **Philippians 2:12-13**, *"...but now much more in my absence, work out your salvation with fear and trembling; for it is God who is at work in you, both to will and to work for His good pleasure."*

Paul again emphasizes this faith of trusting in God in **Colossians 1:29** *"For this purpose also I labor, striving according to His power, which mightily works within me."* Paul labored for Christ, but constantly reminded people that it was God working in him and in them; *"But by the grace of God I am what I am, and His grace toward me did not prove vain; but I labored even more than all of them, yet not I, but the grace of God with me."* **1Corinthians 15:10**

"I have been crucified with Christ; and it is no longer I who live, but Christ lives in me; and the life which I now live in the flesh I live by faith in the Son of God, who loved me and gave Himself up for me." **Galatians 2:20**

Paul also actively sought to know Christ more deeply. He did not strive to know Christ in order to gain a better standing before God. On the contrary, Paul's desire to know Christ was a supernatural response to God's grace being lavished upon him and his being given a righteous standing before God. Paul explained that he did not have a righteousness of his own, but *"...that which is through faith in Christ, the righteousness which comes from God on the basis of faith."* **Philippians 3:9**

Paul declared; *"But whatever things were gain to me, those things I have counted as loss for the sake of Christ. [8] More than that, I count all things to be loss in view of the surpassing value of knowing Christ Jesus my Lord, for whom I have suffered the loss of all things, and count them but rubbish so that I may gain Christ, and may be found in Him, not having a righteousness of my own derived from the Law, but that which is through faith in Christ, the righteousness which comes from God on the basis of faith, that I may know Him and the power of His resurrection...I press on so that I may lay hold of that for which also I was laid hold of by Christ Jesus. ...forgetting what lies behind and reaching forward to what lies ahead, I press on toward the goal for the prize of the upward call of God in Christ Jesus.*" **Philippians 3:7-14**

Made in the USA
Columbia, SC
11 March 2018